LUNCH BOX

LUNCH IDEAS FOR KIDS & ADULTS

THE AUSTRALIAN
Women's Weekly

LUNCH BOX

LUNCH IDEAS FOR KIDS & ADULTS

CONTENTS

Prep and Storage

Home-made always trumps store-bought, and with a little careful planning, you can have a home-made lunch at work or uni every day. This saves you money, plus puts you in control of every ingredient and nutrient you eat.

CHEAP EAT

BIG flavours, low cost. No splurging on a healthy lunch.

MEAT FREE

MEATLESS options for part- and full-time vegetarians.

NUT FREE

REST assured the lunches you send to school have no nuts.

GLUTEN FREE

ESSENTIAL if your health depends on no gluten at all.

5 A DAY

GET maximum goodness with vegie-heavy options.

No one likes, or deserves, a boring lunch. Whether you eat yours hunched over a work computer (tsk tsk), grab it between classes on campus, or you sit and eat it under a shady tree during lunch break, you need a meal full of nourishment and interest. When energy wanes in the late morning, it helps to know that a delicious sandwich, soup or salad is waiting for you. The key is in thinking ahead – decide on next week's lunches over the weekend then shop for them all together, if that's practical.

USE LEFTOVERS

Utilise leftovers (when there are any) from dinner the night before; roast chicken and other meats make excellent sandwich fillings and leftover roast or grilled vegetables can form the basis of a delicious salad, for example. Cook extra food for dinner so you have excess for lunches – extra meats and vegetables for sandwich fillings or extra pasta, rice or other grains for a salad, for example. Get creative; leftover bolognese sauce, curry, home-made baked beans or a meat-based casserole can be baked in puff pastry to make easy hand pies for lunch. Leftover breakfast can also be repurposed for the lunch box; combine cooled, excess porridge with yoghurt, honey and chopped fruits for a nutritious treat. Or roll leftover pancakes around a lightly sweetened ricotta and strawberry filling. The possibilities are endless, with a little creative thinking.

THE FREEZER IS YOUR FRIEND

It's a lifesaver to have lunches frozen, ready to go, and the extent of foods which can be frozen may surprise you. Many prepared sandwiches will freeze, including those filled with grated cheese, peanut butter, ham, salami and roast meats. Mustards, pickles, mayo and chutneys will freeze well too. Pies, quiches, pizza, cakes and sweet slices can be pre-portioned and frozen, and muffins and scones freeze brilliantly too. Have plenty of different types of breads, wraps and rolls on hand in the freezer to make your sandwiches.

DO-AHEAD HACKS

Consider other ways to reduce work by preparing ahead of time; here are just a few. Cut a week's worth of vegetable sticks (to eat with dips) on Sunday; they'll keep all week, portioned in containers. Bake double batches of muffins, cakes, scones, pastries etc. and freeze. Very finely slice root vegetables (beetroot, sweet potato and parsnips) and dry in the oven overnight at a low temperature for healthy crisps. Use your slow cooker or pressure cooker to make big batches of recipes you can use in lunches.

SAFETY and TRANSPORT

LUNCH BOXES COME IN MANY DIFFERENT STYLES AND SIZES, AND IN A RANGE OF MATERIALS, FROM PLASTIC AND NYLON TO STAINLESS STEEL. IT'S IMPORTANT TO HAVE THE RIGHT KIND OF BOX TO PROTECT YOUR FOOD AND KEEP IT SAFELY AT THE RIGHT TEMPERATURE, UNTIL YOU EAT IT.

FOOD SAFETY is the biggest concern with a packed lunch. If it's not stored properly for the few hours before you eat it, bacteria can grow. Meat and dairy products are particularly prone. Other high risk foods include fish, poultry, eggs and anything packaged in a jar or can, which can become high risk once opened. This is especially the case concerning children as little ones can be more susceptible to food poisoning. Keeping foods cool is the key to food safety. If you don't have a lunch box that can be chilled, consider throwing a frozen ice-pack in with your packed box to keep food as cool as possible. Freezing a plastic bottle of water or juice will perform the same function and makes for a refreshingly chilled drink by the time lunchtime comes around too. Even using frozen bread slices for making sandwiches, and packing baked goods straight from the freezer, will keep things chilled for just that extra bit longer. The lowest risk foods for spoilage include uncooked fruits and vegetables, dried foods (crackers, biscuits and other baked goods) and pre-packaged foods such as cereal bars, dried fruits and popcorn.

TYPES OF LUNCH BOXES

What you pack your lunch in is as important as the lunch itself. Squashed sandwiches, leaked salad juices and crushed bananas are depressing scenarios and easily avoided by using a sturdy box. Have a variety of shapes and styles of lunch containers on hand to accommodate different seasons and types of lunch; one size doesn't fit all.

CLASSIC BOXES A good lunch box is not only best for transporting food but is healthy for the environment as well. While a plastic bag may seem an easier option, it's more eco-friendly to use a box that will last for, in many instances, years. Boxes run the gamut of simple, economical supermarket buys to smart canvas bag-like boxes with multiple compartments. What works in summer may not work in winter; for example, boxes with a little ventilation are important for warmer ambient temperatures as food more readily overheats and sweats when tightly enclosed.

BENTO BOXES Boxes with different compartments are excellent when you need to separate your salad from your dips and your cheese from your chocolate cake. With this type of box there is no need to wrap foods, meaning less plastic, which in turn is better for the environment. Stainless steel is a great material as it is sturdy and washes well, without retaining food odours and taints, as plastic can.

THERMOS Invest in a thermos flask to hold food at the right temperature for hours. It will keep soups, casseroles, baked beans etc. hot, and yoghurt, chilled soups and desserts safely cold for up to six hours. Some have two or more stackable compartments, cleverly designed for transporting both hot and chilled dishes at the same time. There are also freezable poly-canvas lunch bags with water-resistant lining, which you freeze overnight. These keep foods fresh for hours, without the hassle of including a separate ice-pack.

SANDWICHES and WRAPS

JAPANESE EGG and CRESS ROLLS

PREP + COOK TIME 25 MINUTES   **MAKES** 2

4 eggs
1 tsp curry powder
¼ cup (75g) japanese
  mayonnaise
2 brioche buns
2 tsp shichimi togarashi
  (optional)
20g cress

1 Place eggs in a saucepan; cover with cold water. Bring to the boil, then turn off heat. Cover with a tight-fitting lid; stand for 15 minutes. Peel; cool.
2 Halve eggs, then chop coarsely; transfer to a bowl. Add curry powder and mayonnaise; season to taste. Stir until well combined.
3 Halve brioche buns horizontally. Divide egg mixture between two bun bases; sprinkle evenly with togarashi. Top each with half the cress and the bun lids.

SWAP IT   Use your favourite mayonnaise instead of the japanese mayonnaise and regular bread rolls instead of the brioche, if preferred.

PREP IT   Make rolls the night before or in the morning.

TAKE IT   Wrap rolls in plastic wrap, or pack in resealable sandwich bags or reusable sandwich containers. Transport in cooler bags. Refrigerate until ready to serve.

CHEAP EAT

Vegie Nachos Wraps

PREP + COOK TIME 25 MINUTES **MAKES** 2

1 tbsp olive oil

½ small red onion (50g),
    chopped finely

1 tbsp burrito spice mix

½ cup finely chopped coriander
    leaves and stems

400g can four-bean mix,
    drained, rinsed

⅓ cup (85g) chunky tomato
    salsa

2 tbsp smoky chipotle sauce

½ cup (60g) grated smoked
    cheese

2 wholegrain wraps

½ cup (40g) finely shredded
    red cabbage

2 tbsp sour cream

¼ cup coriander leaves, extra

GUACAMOLE

1 avocado, mashed

1 clove garlic, crushed

2 tsp sweet chilli sauce

1 tsp lime juice

1 tbsp finely chopped coriander
    leaves and stems

1 Heat oil in a saucepan over medium heat; cook onion for 3 minutes or until softened. Add spice mix and coriander; cook, stirring, for 30 seconds. Add beans, salsa, sauce and cheese; cook, stirring, for 2 minutes. Cool.

2 Meanwhile, make guacamole.

3 Place wraps on a chopping board; spread guacamole down centre of each wrap. Top with bean mixture, cabbage, sour cream and extra coriander. Fold in sides and wrap up tightly to enclose filling; cut in half.

GUACAMOLE Combine ingredients in a small bowl; season to taste.

SWAP IT Use smaller wraps for kids, if you like.

PREP IT Make wraps the night before or in the morning.

TAKE IT Enclose wraps in baking paper tied with kitchen string, plastic wrap or foil, or pack in reusable sandwich containers. Transport in cooler bags. Refrigerate until ready to serve.

Nut Free

Roast chicken, seed and ROCKET SANDWICHES

PREP TIME 10 MINUTES **MAKES** 4

2 cups (340g) chopped barbecued chicken breast
2 cups (100g) baby rocket leaves, chopped
1 trimmed celery stalk, chopped finely
1 cup flat-leaf parsley leaves, chopped finely (see tip)
1 green onion, chopped finely
⅓ cup (50g) natural seed mix (pepitas and sunflower seeds), chopped coarsely
½ cup (150g) whole-egg mayonnaise
2 tbsp lemon juice
8 slices wholemeal bread
40g butter, softened

1 Place chicken, rocket, celery, parsley, green onion, seeds, mayonnaise and lemon juice in a bowl; use a fork to combine. Season to taste.
2 Spread bread slices with butter. Divide chicken mixture among four of the bread slices; top with the remaining bread slices. Cut sandwiches in half.

Tip   You will need about 1 bunch parsley for this recipe.

Swap it   If you have leftover roast chicken, use this instead of barbecued chicken. Use toasted coarsely chopped unsalted pistachios instead of the seed mix, if you like.

Prep it   The filling can be prepared to the end of step 1 up to 2 days in advance and refrigerated in an airtight container. Make sandwiches the night before or in the morning.

Take it   Wrap sandwiches in plastic wrap, or pack in resealable sandwich bags or reusable sandwich containers. Transport in cooler bags. Refrigerate until ready to serve.

MEATBALL SUBS

PREP + COOK TIME 30 MINUTES **MAKES** 6

500g minced beef
1 egg
½ cup (35g) stale breadcrumbs
⅔ cup (50g) finely grated parmesan
⅓ cup chopped flat-leaf parsley
2 tbsp olive oil
1 cup (250ml) tomato pasta sauce
6 long soft bread rolls
60g baby rocket leaves
1 tsp balsamic vinegar (optional)

1 Combine beef, egg, breadcrumbs, half the parmesan and the parsley in a bowl; roll tablespoons of mixture into 24 meatballs.

2 Heat oil in a large deep non-stick frying pan over medium heat; cook meatballs, turning, for 10 minutes or until browned and cooked through.

3 Add pasta sauce to pan; bring to a simmer.

4 Split rolls lengthways from the top, without cutting all the way through. Spread sides with sauce.

5 Combine rocket and vinegar in a small bowl; divide salad among rolls.

6 Fill each roll with four meatballs and scatter with the remaining parmesan.

SWAP IT Use gem or cos lettuce leaves instead of the rocket, if preferred.

PREP IT Meatballs can be prepared to the end of step 3 and refrigerated in an airtight container up to 2 days in advance. Continue from step 4 the night before or in the morning.

TAKE IT Wrap subs in baking paper and pack in airtight containers. Transport in cooler bags. Refrigerate until ready to serve.

CHEAP EAT

'SUSHI' WRAPS TWO WAYS

PREP TIME 15 MINUTES **MAKES** 4 LARGE WRAPS OR 20 PIECES

PASTRAMI, SWISS CHEESE and EASY SLAW WRAPS

125g prepacked classic coleslaw mix
1 tsp dijonnaise
2 mountain bread wraps
100g pastrami
6 slices swiss cheese

1 Combine coleslaw and dijonnaise in a bowl. Top each wrap with half the pastrami and coleslaw mixture; top with cheese.
2 Roll wraps tightly to enclose filling. Cut each wrap crossways into five even pieces to form sandwich 'sushi'.

Tip Use toothpicks to hold the 'sushi' together, if you like.

Swap it Use your favourite mayonnaise instead of dijonnaise, if preferred.

Prep it Wraps can be made in the morning.

Take it Pack 'sushi' into airtight containers, or you can enclose the wraps in baking paper, then foil and cut in half, if preferred. Transport in cooler bags. Refrigerate until ready to serve.

SMOKED SALMON and GOAT'S CHEESE WRAPS

2 mountain bread wraps
60g spring onion and chive goat's cheese or cream cheese spread
100g smoked salmon slices
4 baby gem lettuce leaves, trimmed

1 Spread each wrap with cheese; top each with half the salmon and lettuce.

2 Roll wraps tightly to enclose filling. Cut each wrap crossways into five even pieces to form sandwich 'sushi'.

Swap it Use regular cream cheese instead of flavoured cream cheese or goat's cheese, if preferred.

Prep it Wraps can be made in the morning.

Take it Pack 'sushi' into airtight containers, or you can enclose the wraps in baking paper, then foil and cut in half, if preferred. Transport in cooler bags. Refrigerate until ready to serve.

Nut Free

LEMON GRASS BEEF BANH MI

PREP + COOK TIME 35 MINUTES (+ REFRIGERATION) MAKES 4

¼ cup (75g) whole-egg
   mayonnaise

3 tsp sriracha or other chilli
   sauce (optional)

2 half baguettes, ends trimmed,
   halved crossways

2 baby cucumbers (qukes),
   cut into batons

1 carrot, julienned

1 green onion, cut into
   5cm lengths

8 large fresh coriander sprigs

LEMON GRASS BEEF

300g beef porterhouse or
   rump steak, fat trimmed,
   sliced thinly on the diagonal

1 tbsp fish sauce

1 stalk fresh lemon grass, white
   part only, chopped finely

1 clove garlic, crushed

1 tbsp vegetable oil

1 red shallot, halved,
   sliced thinly

2 tsp white sugar

1 Make lemon grass beef.

2 Combine mayonnaise and chilli sauce in a small bowl.

3 Split baguette pieces lengthways from the top, without cutting all the way through. Spread sides with mayonnaise mixture; fill baguettes evenly with lemon grass beef, cucumber, carrot, green onion and coriander. Drizzle with extra mayonnaise mixture.

LEMON GRASS BEEF Place beef, fish sauce, half the lemon grass and half the garlic in a bowl; stir to mix well. Refrigerate, covered, for at least 30 minutes for flavours to develop. Heat a wok or large heavy-based frying pan over high heat. Add half the oil; stir-fry beef for 4 minutes or until browned. Transfer to a plate. Heat remaining oil in wok; stir-fry shallot, remaining lemon grass and garlic for 2 minutes or until fragrant. Return beef to wok, then add sugar; stir-fry to combine for 30 seconds. Season to taste with pepper.

SWAP IT Use chicken breast fillet instead of steak; stir-fry until cooked through. Use one long baguette cut into quarters instead of half baguettes, if preferred.

PREP IT The lemon grass beef can be made up to 2 days in advance and refrigerated in an airtight container. Make banh mi the night before or in the morning.

TAKE IT Wrap banh mi in baking paper or pack in airtight containers. Transport in cooler bags. Refrigerate until ready to serve.

Tikka Paneer Wraps

PREP + COOK TIME 15 MINUTES   **MAKES** 2

200g paneer cheese, cut into
    8 slices crossways

2 tbsp tikka masala paste

1 tbsp olive oil

2 spinach and herb wraps

50g baby kale leaves

1 small lebanese cucumber,
    sliced thinly into ribbons

1 small carrot, julienned

1 green onion, sliced

RAITA

½ small lebanese cucumber,
    grated coarsely

¼ cup (70g) Greek-style yoghurt

2 tbsp mint leaves, shredded

¼ tsp ground cumin

1 Coat paneer with tikka paste. Heat oil in a heavy-based non-stick frying pan over medium-high heat; cook paneer, turning, for 2 minutes or until golden. Set aside to cool.

2 Make raita.

3 Lay wraps on a chopping board; top with kale, cucumber, paneer, carrot, green onion and raita. Fold in sides and wrap up tightly to enclose filling; cut wraps in half.

RAITA Squeeze as much liquid from the grated cucumber as possible. Add to yoghurt with mint and cumin; stir to combine. Season to taste. Makes ⅓ cup.

Swap it We used 25cm diameter wraps here; use smaller wraps for kids, if you like.

Prep it Make wraps the night before or in the morning.

Take it Enclose wraps in baking paper tied with kitchen string, plastic wrap or foil, or pack in reusable sandwich containers. Transport in cooler bags. Refrigerate until ready to serve.

MEAT FREE

Twisted Tuna Rolls

TUNA and AVOCADO CAESAR SALAD ROLL

PREP TIME 10 MINUTES   **MAKES** 1

Mix a drained 125g can tuna in oil with 1 tbsp caesar dressing and 1 tsp finely grated parmesan. Butter a bread roll. Top base with baby cos leaves, then tuna mixture, sliced avocado and sliced ripe tomato. Season to taste; serve. Add crisp prosciutto, if you like.

TUNA 'SUSHI' SUB

PREP TIME 10 MINUTES   **MAKES** 1

Mix a drained 125g can tuna in oil with 1 tbsp japanese mayonnaise and sriracha chilli sauce to taste. Butter a split long crusty bread roll. Fill roll with lebanese cucumber ribbons, tuna mixture and thinly sliced radish. Season to taste; serve.

TUNA and ROASTED CAPSICUM SUB

PREP TIME 10 MINUTES   **MAKES** 1

Mix a drained 125g can tuna in oil with 1 tbsp aïoli, 2 tsp finely chopped basil and 2 tsp chopped toasted pine nuts or sunflower seeds (or 2 tsp pesto instead of the basil and pine nuts). Butter a split long crusty bread roll. Fill roll with trimmed rocket leaves and tuna mixture; top with drained marinated capsicum strips. Season to taste; serve.

MEXICAN TUNA SALAD ROLL

PREP TIME 10 MINUTES   **MAKES** 1

Mix a drained 125g can tuna in oil with 1 tbsp whole-egg mayonnaise, a little finely chopped red onion, finely chopped coriander, 1 tbsp drained canned corn and chipotle Tabasco sauce to taste. Butter a ciabatta bread roll. Top base with watercress, then tuna mixture and coriander leaves. Season to taste; serve.

JAPANESE OMELETTE WRAPS

PREP + COOK TIME 40 MINUTES (+ REFRIGERATION) **MAKES** 2

½ cup (100g) sushi rice

1 tbsp vegetable oil

130g orange sweet potato, grated coarsely (see tips)

1 green onion, chopped finely

4 large eggs, beaten lightly

¼ cup coriander leaves

4 baby gem lettuce leaves, trimmed

MARINATED TOFU

2 tbsp rice wine vinegar

1 tbsp tamari

1 tbsp mirin

1 tbsp sesame oil

1 tsp caster sugar

2 tsp finely chopped coriander stems

90g firm tofu, halved lengthways, cut into 5mm-thick slices

1 Cook sushi rice following packet directions. Transfer to a bowl and cover; refrigerate until needed.

2 Make marinated tofu.

3 Cut two 30cm squares of baking paper and two of foil. Top each sheet of foil with a sheet of paper for wrapping.

4 Heat oil in a 26cm non-stick frying pan over medium heat. Cook potato and onion, stirring frequently, for 3 minutes or until softened slightly. Add 2 tablespoons of the tofu marinade to pan; cook for a further 1 minute or until liquid is evaporated. Remove half the sweet potato mixture from the pan; set aside until needed. Spread remaining sweet potato mixture evenly over base of pan.

5 Pour half the egg into the frying pan; tilt to spread to the edges. Cook egg, without stirring, for 2 minutes or until egg just sets. Carefully slide omelette onto one sheet of prepared paper. Repeat with remaining sweet potato mixture and egg to make a second omelette. Refrigerate omelettes until cool.

6 Place half the rice in a log across the centre of each omelette; top with half the coriander, drained marinated tofu and lettuce leaves. Using the paper and foil underneath, wrap omelettes up tightly, squeezing the ends to seal as you go; cut wraps in half.

MARINATED TOFU Combine vinegar, tamari, mirin, sesame oil, sugar and coriander in a bowl. Add tofu; stir to cover in dressing. Cover; refrigerate for up to 4 days.

Swap it Use shredded cooked chicken meat instead of tofu for a non-vegetarian version.

Prep it Make wraps the night before or in the morning.

Take it Enclose wraps in baking paper tied with kitchen string, plastic wrap or foil. Transport in cooler bags. Refrigerate until ready to serve.

Gluten Free

Greek salad lamb pitta pockets

PREP + COOK TIME 25 MINUTES MAKES 4

250g lamb backstraps

1 tbsp olive oil

1 tsp dried oregano

½ tsp ground sumac

4 pitta pockets

250g baby cucumbers (qukes), sliced thinly into ribbons

2 roma tomatoes, sliced

1 baby gem lettuce, leaves separated

80g kalamata olives, pitted, halved

WHIPPED FETTA

200g danish fetta

1 cup mint leaves

2 tbsp lemon juice

1 tbsp extra virgin olive oil

1 Place lamb in a small bowl; rub well with oil, oregano and sumac. Season.

2 Preheat a large non-stick frying pan over medium heat. Cook lamb for 4 minutes on each side for medium-rare or until cooked to your liking. Cover loosely with foil; cool. Slice thinly; refrigerate if not using immediately.

3 Make whipped fetta.

4 Warm the pitta pockets in microwave to refresh. Split pitta pockets open; spread a quarter of the whipped fetta inside each one. Divide cucumber, tomato, lettuce, olives and lamb among pockets; season with pepper to taste.

WHIPPED FETTA Process ingredients in a small food processor until well combined and completely smooth. Makes 1 cup.

Swap it If you have any leftover roast lamb, use this instead of cooking the lamb backstraps. Instead of making the whipped fetta, you can use purchased spreadable fetta, fetta dip or tzatziki, if you like.

Prep it Make pitta pockets the night before or in the morning.

Take it Wrap pitta pockets in plastic wrap or foil, or pack in airtight containers. Alternatively, pack pitta pockets, lamb, salad ingredients and whipped fetta in separate airtight containers to assemble at work. Transport in cooler bags. Refrigerate until ready to serve.

TERIYAKI CHICKEN SALAD ROLLS

PREP + COOK TIME 25 MINUTES   **MAKES** 4

500g chicken tenderloins

¼ cup (60ml) teriyaki marinade

1 baguette, cut into quarters

8 inner baby cos lettuce
  leaves, trimmed

1 large avocado, sliced thinly

2 lebanese cucumbers, sliced
  thinly into ribbons

1 tbsp lemon juice

¼ cup mint leaves

MISO AVOCADO SPREAD

1 medium avocado (250g),
  chopped

¼ cup (75g) japanese
  mayonnaise

3 tsp white (shiro) miso

1 Place chicken and teriyaki marinade in a medium bowl; mix to coat chicken well.

2 Heat a grill plate (or grill pan) over medium heat; line with baking paper. Cook chicken for 4 minutes on each side or until cooked through. Transfer to a plate; cover loosely with foil to keep warm, if serving straight away.

3 Make miso avocado spread.

4 Meanwhile, split baguette pieces lengthways, without cutting all the way through. Spread bases with miso avocado spread; top with lettuce, avocado, chicken, cucumber and extra miso avocado spread. Drizzle with lemon juice; scatter with mint.

MISO AVOCADO SPREAD Process ingredients in a food processor until smooth; season to taste.

SWAP IT For a spicier version, use your favourite chilli sauce instead of the teriyaki marinade. Use your favourite mayonnaise instead of japanese mayonnaise in the miso avocado spread, if preferred. Alternatively, skip making the spread and use your favourite purchased aïoli or avocado dip.

PREP IT The chicken can be prepared to the end of step 2 up to 2 days in advance and refrigerated in an airtight container. Make the rolls the night before or in the morning. Add the avocado just before serving, if preferred.

TAKE IT Wrap rolls in baking paper tied with kitchen string, plastic wrap or foil, or pack in airtight containers. Transport in cooler bags. Refrigerate until ready to serve.

CHEAP EAT

Smoked Turkey and Brie Sandwiches

PREP TIME 10 MINUTES **MAKES** 2

4 slices light rye bread
1 tbsp cranberry sauce
50g brie, sliced thinly
1 cup (50g) baby spinach leaves
1 large vine-ripened tomato,
    sliced thinly
80g smoked turkey slices
1½ tbsp whole-egg mayonnaise
1 tsp dijon mustard

1 Lay bread slices on a chopping board. Divide cranberry sauce, brie, spinach, tomato and turkey between two of the bread slices. Season to taste.
2 Combine mayonnaise and dijon mustard in a small bowl.
3 Spread remaining bread slices with the dijon mayonnaise and place on top of filling; cut sandwiches in half.

Swap It Use plum paste instead of cranberry sauce, if preferred. Use dijonnaise instead of combining the mayonnaise and dijon mustard yourself.

Prep It Make sandwiches in the morning.

Take It Wrap sandwiches in plastic wrap, or pack in resealable sandwich bags or reusable sandwich containers. Transport in cooler bags. Refrigerate until ready to serve.

Roast beef, artichoke and Tuna aïoli baguettes

PREP TIME 15 MINUTES **SERVES** 4

1 baguette, cut into quarters

8 slices purchased roast beef

8 drained quartered artichoke
hearts

¼ cup flat-leaf parsley leaves

TUNA AÏOLI

½ cup (150g) aïoli

95g can tuna in oil, drained

4 anchovy fillets, chopped

1 tbsp lemon juice

2 tsp baby capers

⅓ cup flat-leaf parsley leaves,
sliced thinly

1 Make tuna aïoli.

2 Split baguette pieces lengthways from the top, without cutting all the way through. Spread sides with tuna aïoli; fill with roast beef, artichoke and parsley. Drizzle with extra tuna aïoli.

TUNA AÏOLI Process ingredients until smooth; season. Transfer to an airtight container; refrigerate until needed.

Swap it If you have any leftover roast beef, use this instead of purchasing sliced roast beef. Use drained marinated capsicum, rocket leaves or sliced tomato instead of artichokes, if preferred. Omit making the tuna aïoli and use regular aïoli or your favourite purchased flavoured mayonnaise instead.

Prep it Tuna aïoli can be made up to 3 days in advance and refrigerated in an airtight container. Make the baguettes the night before or in the morning.

Take it Wrap baguettes in baking paper or plastic wrap, or pack in airtight containers. Alternatively, pack baguettes, roast beef, artichokes and aïoli in separate airtight containers to assemble at work. Transport in cooler bags. Refrigerate until ready to serve.

MEAT FREE

Middle Eastern Cauli-Lentil Burgers

PREP + COOK TIME 30 MINUTES (+ REFRIGERATION) **MAKES** 4

200g cauliflower, chopped coarsely

400g can lentils, drained, rinsed

2 tsp ground cumin

2 tsp ground coriander

2 tbsp sunflower seeds

2 tbsp chopped coriander leaves and stems

2 cloves garlic, crushed

1 egg

½ cup (50g) fresh breadcrumbs

2 tbsp plain flour

oil, for shallow-frying

4 hamburger buns

60g baby rocket leaves

1 small carrot, sliced thinly into ribbons

1 small lebanese cucumber, sliced thinly into ribbons

TZATZIKI SAUCE

½ small lebanese cucumber, grated coarsely

⅓ cup (95g) Greek-style yoghurt

⅓ cup mint leaves, chopped

2 tsp lemon juice

¼ tsp chilli powder (optional)

1 Process cauliflower, lentils, spices, seeds, chopped coriander, garlic, egg and breadcrumbs until just combined. Transfer mixture to a large bowl; season, then fold in flour.

2 Using floured hands, divide mixture into four patties. Place on a lined tray; refrigerate for 20 minutes to firm.

3 Meanwhile, make tzatziki sauce.

4 Heat oil in a non-stick heavy-based frying pan over medium heat; cook patties, in batches, for 3 minutes on each side or until golden. Drain on paper towel.

5 Split buns; top bases with rocket, patties, tzatziki sauce, carrot, cucumber and bun lids.

TZATZIKI SAUCE Squeeze excess liquid from grated cucumber. Combine with remaining ingredients in a small bowl; season to taste. Makes about ½ cup.

Swap it Use your favourite purchased tzatziki instead of making the tzatziki sauce, if preferred.

Prep it Recipe can be made to the end of step 4 up to 2 days in advance; refrigerate patties and tzatziki sauce in separate airtight containers. Make burgers the night before or in the morning.

Take it Wrap burgers in baking paper or plastic wrap, or pack in airtight containers. Transport in cooler bags. Refrigerate until ready to serve.

JAFFLES
and MELTS

REUBEN JAFFLES

PREP + COOK TIME 10 MINUTES MAKES 2

4 slices light rye bread

30g butter, softened

2 tsp pistachio dukkah (optional)

8 slices swiss cheese

6 slices pastrami

⅓ cup (35g) purchased sauerkraut

2 tbsp thousand island dressing

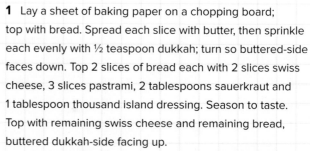

1 Lay a sheet of baking paper on a chopping board; top with bread. Spread each slice with butter, then sprinkle each evenly with ½ teaspoon dukkah; turn so buttered-side faces down. Top 2 slices of bread each with 2 slices swiss cheese, 3 slices pastrami, 2 tablespoons sauerkraut and 1 tablespoon thousand island dressing. Season to taste. Top with remaining swiss cheese and remaining bread, buttered dukkah-side facing up.

2 Preheat a jaffle maker. Toast sandwiches in hot jaffle maker for 4 minutes or until cheese melts and bread is crisp and golden.

Swap It   Use purchased roast beef or ham instead of pastrami, if preferred.

Prep It   Assemble sandwiches to the end of step 1 the night before or in the morning.

Take It   Wrap sandwiches in baking paper and pack in reusable sandwich containers. Transport in cooler bags. Refrigerate until ready to toast. Continue with step 2.

CHEAP EAT

Nut
Free

L₁ U₁ N₁ C₃ H₄

CHEESY CHORIZO QUESADITAS

PREP + COOK TIME 20 MINUTES MAKES 2

1 tbsp olive oil

1 small red onion, chopped finely

2 cured chorizos, chopped finely

1 tsp smoked paprika

⅓ cup (80g) chopped drained roasted red capsicum

2 wholemeal pitta pockets

1 cup (100g) grated four cheese mix

30g baby spinach leaves

1 Heat oil in a medium frying pan over medium-high heat; cook onion, stirring, for 3 minutes or until softened. Add chorizo; cook for 2 minutes or until golden. Add paprika; cook for 30 seconds. Stir in capsicum; season to taste.

2 Warm the pitta pockets in microwave to refresh. Split pitta pockets open. Fill each with a quarter of the cheese, half the chorizo mixture and half the spinach, then top with remaining cheese.

3 Preheat a sandwich press; toast quesaditas in hot sandwich press for 4 minutes or until golden and crisp.

PREP IT The filling can be prepared to the end of step 1 the night before and refrigerated in an airtight container. Assemble quesaditas to the end of step 2 the night before or in the morning.

TAKE IT Wrap quesaditas in baking paper and pack in airtight containers. Alternatively, pack ingredients in separate airtight containers to assemble at work. Transport in cooler bags. Refrigerate until ready to toast. Continue with step 3.

JAPANESE CHICKEN SCHNITZEL TOASTIES

PREP + COOK TIME 20 MINUTES (+ COOLING) **MAKES** 2

oil, for shallow-frying

1 purchased crumbed
   chicken schnitzel (110g)

1 cup (80g) finely shredded
   wombok

1 tbsp rice wine vinegar

4 slices seeded bread

30g butter, softened

4 slices colby cheese

miso avocado spread, to serve
   (see page 32)

1 Heat oil in a non-stick frying pan over medium heat. Cook schnitzel for 4 minutes on each side or until crisp, golden and cooked through. Drain on paper towel. Cool; slice thinly.

2 Combine wombok and vinegar in a small bowl; season.

3 Lay a sheet of baking paper on a chopping board; top with bread. Spread each slice with butter; turn so buttered-side faces down. Top 2 slices of bread each with 2 slices of cheese, half the schnitzel and half the wombok mixture. Top with remaining bread, buttered-side up.

4 Preheat a sandwich press; toast sandwiches in hot sandwich press for 5 minutes or until cheese melts and bread is golden and crisp. Serve toasties with miso avocado spread.

SWAP IT   Make the chicken katsu on page 99 and use here instead of buying ready-made schnitzel, if preferred. Alternatively, you can use purchased pork schnitzel instead of the chicken, if you like.

PREP IT   Assemble sandwiches to the end of step 3 the night before or in the morning.

TAKE IT   Wrap sandwiches in baking paper and pack in reusable sandwich containers. Alternatively, pack buttered bread, schnitzel, wombok and miso avocado spread in separate airtight containers to assemble at work. Transport in cooler bags. Refrigerate until ready to toast. Continue with step 4.

CHEAP EAT

CHEAP
EAT

SALAMI, CHEESE and PESTO MELTS

PREP + COOK TIME 10 MINUTES   **MAKES** 2

2 long slices olive sourdough
  bread
2 tbsp purchased pesto
1 vine-ripened tomato, sliced
180g drained marinated
  artichoke hearts, sliced
50g sliced salami
1 cup (100g) grated mozzarella

1 Preheat an oven griller.

2 Toast bread for 1 minute on each side or until golden.
Spread one side of each slice with 1 tablespoon of pesto;
top with half each of the tomato, artichoke and salami.

3 Scatter each slice with half the mozzarella; place
under hot grill for 3 minutes or until golden and bubbling.
Season to taste.

TIP Top with bread slices to make toasties instead of melts.

SWAP IT Use mortadella, ham or prosciutto instead of
salami, if you like.

TAKE IT Pack ingredients in separate airtight containers
to assemble at work. Transport in cooler bags. Refrigerate
until ready to make. If you don't have a griller at work,
you can toast the melts in a hot sandwich press lined with
baking paper.

SALMON and KIMCHI BRIOCHE TOASTIES

PREP + COOK TIME 10 MINUTES **MAKES** 2

1 tbsp japanese mayonnaise

2 brioche rolls, split

2 tbsp kimchi

2 small red radishes,
  sliced thinly

2 green onions, chopped finely

100g wood-roasted smoked
  salmon portion, flaked

2 tbsp coarsely chopped
  coriander

½ cup (50g) grated mozzarella

shichimi togarashi, to sprinkle

1 Spread mayonnaise over brioche bases; top with kimchi, radish, green onion, salmon, coriander, mozzarella and brioche lids. Sprinkle with togarashi to form a light coating.

2 Preheat a sandwich press. Toast brioche in hot sandwich press for 2 minutes or until toasted, golden and cheese is melted.

SWAP IT Use regular mayonnaise instead of japanese mayonnaise and a well-drained 95g can salmon instead of wood-roasted salmon, if preferred.

PREP IT Assemble brioche rolls to the end of step 1 the night before or in the morning.

TAKE IT Pack brioche rolls in airtight containers. Alternatively, pack ingredients in separate airtight containers to assemble at work. Transport in cooler bags. Refrigerate until ready to toast. Continue with step 2.

Nut Free

MEXICAN HAM and CREAMED CORN JAFFLES

PREP + COOK TIME 20 MINUTES   MAKES 2

1 tbsp olive oil

1 small red capsicum, chopped finely

2 jalapeño chillies, seeded, chopped finely (optional)

150g shaved leg ham, chopped coarsely

1 tbsp finely chopped coriander stems

½ tsp smoked paprika

¼ tsp ground cumin

125g can creamed corn

1 tbsp finely chopped coriander leaves

1 tsp finely grated lime rind

4 slices white bread

20g butter, softened

1 cup (120g) grated cheddar

mexican hot sauce and lime wedges, to serve (optional)

1 Heat oil in a frying pan over medium heat. Cook capsicum and jalapeño for 2 minutes. Add ham; cook, stirring, for 1 minute. Add coriander stem and spices; cook for 1 minute. Cool slightly.

2 Stir through creamed corn, chopped coriander and rind; season to taste.

3 Lay a sheet of baking paper on a chopping board; top with bread. Spread each slice with butter; turn so buttered-side faces down. Scatter 2 slices of bread with half the cheese; top with half the ham filling and remaining cheese. Top with remaining bread, buttered-side up.

4 Grease a jaffle maker generously with butter and preheat. Toast sandwiches in hot jaffle maker for 2 minutes or until cheese melts and filling is hot.

5 Serve jaffles with mexican hot sauce and lime wedges.

TIP   This makes 1½ cups of filling, so these jaffles are generously filled; divide the filling among 8 slices of bread to make four jaffles, if preferred.

SWAP IT   Instead of the ham, use 150g shredded barbecued chicken, or omit the meat entirely and use another 125g can creamed corn for a vegetarian version.

PREP IT   Assemble sandwiches to the end of step 3 the night before or in the morning.

TAKE IT   Wrap sandwiches in baking paper and pack in reusable sandwich containers. Alternatively, pack buttered bread, filling and cheese in separate airtight containers to assemble at work. Transport in cooler bags. Refrigerate until ready to toast. Continue from step 4.

Moroccan Chicken 'Waldorf' Toasties

PREP + COOK TIME *20 MINUTES* **MAKES** *4*

1 tbsp extra virgin olive oil

2 tbsp tomato paste

1 tsp ground cumin

1 tsp ground coriander

1 tsp ground cinnamon

180g chargrilled capsicum strips, drained, sliced thinly

2 tsp honey

1 cup (150g) cooked chicken, chopped coarsely

2 trimmed celery stalks, chopped coarsely

¼ cup (35g) sunflower seeds, chopped coarsely

¼ cup (70g) Greek-style yoghurt

2 tsp mint leaves, chopped finely

30g red grapes, quartered

8 slices wholemeal sourdough bread

40g butter, softened

1 Heat oil in a small heavy-based saucepan over medium heat. Cook tomato paste and spices, stirring frequently, for 1 minute to form a paste or until just starting to catch on the base of the pan. Add capsicum and honey; cook, stirring, for a further 1 minute. Season to taste; cool.

2 Place capsicum mixture, chicken, celery, seeds, yoghurt and mint in a large bowl; stir to combine. Stir in grapes gently.

3 Toast bread; spread with butter. Top 4 bread slices with chicken mixture, then remaining bread slices.

SWAP IT Use coarsely chopped walnuts instead of sunflower seeds, if preferred. Skip toasting the bread and use your favourite fresh sandwich bread.

PREP IT Make toasties in the morning.

TAKE IT Pack toasties in reusable sandwich containers. Alternatively, pack buttered bread and filling in separate airtight containers to assemble at work and toast in a hot sandwich press. Transport in cooler bags. Refrigerate until ready to serve.

CHEAP
EAT

TIP Chickpea, quinoa and beetroot wraps are available from some major supermarkets and health food stores; use your favourite wrap, if preferred.

FAST MEXICAN BEAN and CHEDDAR BURRITOS

PREP + COOK TIME 10 MINUTES **MAKES** 2

2 chickpea, quinoa and
   beetroot wraps (see tip)
⅓ cup (85g) chunky
   tomato salsa
425g can mexe beans
½ cup (60g) coarsely grated
   cheddar

1 Spread each wrap with half the tomato salsa. Top each with half the beans and cheddar. Season to taste; fold over to enclose filling.

2 Preheat a sandwich press. Toast burritos in hot sandwich press for 3 minutes or until golden and cheese melts.

PREP IT Assemble wraps to the end of step 1 in the morning.

TAKE IT Enclose wraps in baking paper and pack in airtight containers. Transport in cooler bags. Refrigerate until ready to toast. Continue with step 2. Alternatively, you can also eat the burrito untoasted.

SERVE IT Serve with sliced avocado and cherry tomatoes, drizzled with lemon juice and seasoned with pepper.

MEAT FREE

Mix & Melt

ASPARAGUS CROQUE MADAME

PREP + COOK TIME 15 MINUTES
MAKES 1

Blanch 3 asparagus spears in a saucepan of boiling water; drain. Grill 1 brioche slice under a hot griller for 1 minute on each side or until golden. Spread toasted brioche with butter and dijon mustard. Top with 2 slices ham, asparagus and 2 slices swiss or edam cheese. Grill for 1 minute or until cheese melts. Top with a halved soft-boiled egg. Season to taste with pepper.

ZUCCHINI and HALOUMI

PREP + COOK TIME 10 MINUTES
MAKES 1

Brush the cut sides of 1 halved bagel with extra virgin olive oil. Grill under a hot griller for 1 minute on the cut sides or until golden. Top with thinly sliced zucchini and thickly sliced haloumi; drizzle with oil. Grill for 1 minute or until golden; top with mint leaves, finely chopped fresh red chilli (optional) and a drizzle of olive oil. Season with pepper.

JAMON and FIG

PREP + COOK TIME 5 MINUTES
MAKES 1

Brush 1 slice soy and linseed sourdough bread with extra virgin olive oil. Grill under a hot griller for 1 minute on each side or until golden. Top with crumbled goat's cheese; scatter with rosemary leaves. Grill for 1 minute or until cheese melts; top with jamon (or prosciutto), sliced fig and extra goat's cheese. Season to taste.

CAPRESE WITH PESTO

PREP + COOK TIME 5 MINUTES
MAKES 1

Rub 1 small pitta bread round with cut garlic; brush with extra virgin olive oil. Grill under a hot griller for 1 minute on each side or until golden. Top with sliced bocconcini and halved cherry tomatoes. Grill for 1 minute or until cheese melts. Top with pesto and basil leaves. Season to taste.

SWAP IT Instead of making the adobo mayonnaise, serve toasties with purchased chipotle aïoli or peri peri whole-egg mayonnaise.

EAT

'EMPANADA' TOASTIES

PREP + COOK TIME 35 MINUTES   MAKES 6

1 egg
⅓ cup (80ml) olive oil
1 small onion, chopped finely
2 cloves garlic, crushed
½ tsp sweet paprika
½ tsp ground coriander
½ tsp ground cumin
½ tsp dried oregano
225g lean minced beef
2 vine-ripened tomatoes,
   chopped finely
⅓ cup (50g) pimento-stuffed
   green olives, chopped finely
12 sheets fillo pastry
1 cup (120g) grated cheddar

ADOBO MAYONNAISE
½ cup (150g) whole-egg
   mayonnaise
1 tbsp chipotle chillies
   in adobo sauce

1 Cook egg in a saucepan of boiling water for 9 minutes; cool. Peel and chop coarsely.

2 Heat 1 tablespoon of the oil in a frying pan over high heat. Add onion; cook, stirring, for 2 minutes. Add garlic, paprika, coriander, cumin and oregano; cook for a further 1 minute. Add beef mince; cook, stirring to break up lumps, for 3 minutes or until browned and cooked through. Add tomato; cook, stirring, for 2 minutes or until liquid is evaporated.

3 Remove pan from heat; stir through egg and olives. Season; cool slightly to prevent pastry from becoming soggy.

4 Make adobo mayonnaise.

5 Layer 2 rectangular sheets of pastry, brushing each sheet with oil, on a clean surface. Place ¼ cup beef mixture and 2 tablespoons of cheese in a corner of the pastry sheet. Fold opposite corner of pastry across filling to form a triangle; fold any excess pastry over and tuck under triangle. Repeat with remaining pastry, oil, beef mixture and cheese to make a total of 6 'empanadas'.

6 Preheat a sandwich press. Brush each 'empanada' with oil; cook in hot sandwich press for 7 minutes or until golden and crisp.

7 Cut 'empanada' toasties in half and serve with adobo mayonnaise and coriander leaves, if you like.

ADOBO MAYONNAISE Process ingredients in a small food processor until combined.

PREP IT 'Empanada' toasties can be cooked to the end of step 6 the night before. You can also freeze them for up to 1 month; thaw in the fridge.

TAKE IT Wrap toasties in baking paper or plastic wrap. Transport in cooler bags. Refrigerate until ready to serve. Reheat in an oiled sandwich press, if you like.

PROSCIUTTO and PARMESAN SANDWICH PRESS PIZZAS

PREP + COOK TIME 10 MINUTES MAKES 2

2 x 24cm purchased
  pizza bases
2 x 50g pizza sauce sachets
150g mozzarella, sliced thinly
100g prosciutto slices
30g baby rocket leaves
⅓ cup (25g) shaved parmesan
extra virgin olive oil, for drizzling
  (optional)

1 Place pizza bases on a clean work surface; spread each one with half the pizza sauce. Top with mozzarella.

2 Preheat a sandwich press; toast in hot sandwich press lined with baking paper for 2 minutes or until golden.

3 Top pizzas with prosciutto, rocket and parmesan; drizzle with oil. Season to taste.

Swap it While serving-sized sachets of pizza sauce are easy to transport for those taking this to work, you could also use the same weight of tomato pizza sauce paste, available in squeeze bottles from supermarkets. Use ham, salami or pepperoni instead of prosciutto, if preferred.

Prep it For school lunch boxes, make pizzas in the morning and cut into slices.

Take it Pack sliced pizza in airtight containers. Alternatively, pack ingredients in separate airtight containers to assemble at work. Transport in cooler bags. Refrigerate until ready to make.

Cheap Eat

RICOTTA-PEA SMASH and HAM MELTS

PREP + COOK TIME 20 MINUTES   MAKES 8

2 cups (240g) frozen peas

1 cup (150g) frozen broad
  beans, thawed, shelled

1 cup mint leaves

¾ cup (180g) soft ricotta

½ cup (40g) grated parmesan

2 tsp finely grated lemon rind

8 slices sourdough bread

1 tbsp extra virgin olive oil

200g shaved ham

⅔ cup (65g) grated mozzarella

1 Cook peas and broad beans in a saucepan of boiling water for 1 minute or until just tender. Drain, refresh in iced water; drain again. Reserve a quarter of the peas and broad beans.

2 To make the ricotta-pea smash, process remaining peas and broad beans, mint, ricotta, parmesan and lemon rind in a small food processor until smooth. Transfer to a small bowl; stir through reserved peas and beans. Season to taste.

3 Meanwhile, preheat oven griller to medium heat. Line an oven tray with foil.

4 Place bread on lined tray; drizzle evenly with oil. Grill for 2 minutes on each side or until bread is light golden. Top toast with pea mixture, ham and mozzarella; grill for 3 minutes or until cheese is golden and melted. Alternatively, toast melt in a hot sandwich press lined with baking paper until cheese is golden. Season to taste with pepper.

TIP Top melts with bread slices to make toasties or jaffles.

SWAP IT Use salami or prosciutto instead of shaved ham, if you like

PREP IT The ricotta-pea smash can be made to the end of step 2 up to 2 days in advance and refrigerated in an airtight container.

TAKE IT Pack oiled bread, ricotta-pea smash, ham and mozzarella in separate airtight containers to assemble at work. Transport in cooler bags. Refrigerate until ready to make.

CHEAP EAT

Cheat's Spinach *and* CHEESE GOZLEME

PREP + COOK TIME *20 MINUTES* **MAKES** *2*

2 tsp olive oil

1 small red onion, chopped finely

1 clove garlic, crushed

200g baby spinach leaves, chopped coarsely

1 egg, beaten lightly

200g fetta, crumbled

1½ tbsp finely grated parmesan

2 tsp finely grated lemon rind

2 tbsp coarsely chopped dill

4 wholegrain tortillas

⅓ cup (95g) tzatziki (optional)

1 Heat oil in a large heavy-based non-stick frying pan over medium heat. Cook onion, garlic and spinach, stirring, for 2 minutes or until softened. Transfer to a large bowl; cool slightly.

2 Add egg, fetta, parmesan, rind and dill to spinach mixture. Season with pepper; mix well to combine.

3 Divide spinach mixture between two of the tortillas; spread to cover. Top with remaining tortillas.

4 Preheat a sandwich press; toast gozleme in hot sandwich press for 3 minutes or until cooked through and golden.

5 Cut gozleme into wedges; season. Serve with tzatziki.

PREP IT Prepare the recipe to the end of step 3 the night before or in the morning.

TAKE IT Wrap gozleme in baking paper or plastic wrap, or pack in an airtight container. Transport in cooler bags. Refrigerate until ready to toast. Continue from step 4.

SERVE IT Serve gozleme with a cherry tomato and cucumber salad, drizzled with olive oil and lemon juice.

MEAT FREE

CREAMY MUSHROOM and BRIE TOASTIES

PREP + COOK TIME 20 MINUTES **MAKES** 4

¾ cup (190g) mascarpone

2 tsp dijon mustard

4 large portobello mushrooms,
 stalks removed

1 tbsp thyme leaves

1 tbsp extra virgin olive oil

8 slices brioche

50g butter, softened slightly

200g brie, cut into 12 slices

1 Combine mascarpone and mustard in a small bowl, then season; mix until smooth and combined.

2 Halve each mushroom through the middle horizontally; place two halves in a hot sandwich press; top with a quarter of the thyme and brush with 1 teaspoon of the oil; cook for 4 minutes or until mushrooms are just cooked through. Repeat with remaining mushrooms, thyme and oil.

3 Lay a sheet of baking paper on a chopping board; top with brioche. Spread each slice with butter; turn so buttered-side faces down.

4 Remove mushroom halves from sandwich press; place two pieces each on 4 brioche slices. (Do not clean the sandwich press; the mushroom juices will add flavour when toasting the sandwiches in step 6.) Top mushrooms each with 3 cheese slices.

5 Spread mascarpone mixture on remaining brioche slices and place on top of cheese, buttered-side up.

6 Toast sandwiches in hot sandwich press for 4 minutes or until golden and crisp, pressing down lightly.

Prep it Assemble sandwiches to the end of step 5 the night before or in the morning. Alternatively, prepare the mascarpone and mustard mixture, mix the mushrooms with thyme and olive oil, butter the brioche slices and slice the brie; refrigerate separately.

Take it Wrap sandwiches in baking paper, then pack in resealable sandwich bags or reusable sandwich containers. Alternatively, pack brioche and filling ingredients in separate airtight containers to assemble at work. Transport in cooler bags. Refrigerate until ready to toast.

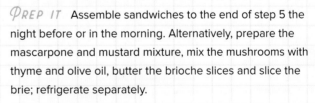

SATISFYING SALADS

LENTIL, FETTA and BEETROOT SALAD

PREP + COOK TIME 30 MINUTES (+ COOLING) SERVES 4

½ cup (100g) French-style
   green lentils

250g packet microwave brown
   rice and quinoa

½ small red onion, chopped
   finely

¼ cup (40g) seed mix (pepitas
   and sunflower seeds), toasted

2 tbsp dried currants

125g vacuum-packed cooked
   beetroot, cut into wedges

125g marinated fetta, drained

60g rocket leaves

HONEY-LEMON DRESSING

¼ cup (60ml) extra virgin
   olive oil

¼ cup (60ml) lemon juice

2 tsp honey

1 tsp ground cumin

1 Cook lentils in a small saucepan of boiling water for 20 minutes or until just tender. Drain, then rinse under cold water; drain well.

2 Meanwhile, prepare brown rice and quinoa following packet directions. Transfer to a large bowl; cool.

3 Make honey-lemon dressing.

4 Add lentils, onion, seed mix, currants, beetroot and crumbled fetta to rice. Season with salt and pepper; top with rocket.

5 Add dressing to salad just before serving. Season.

HONEY-LEMON DRESSING Place ingredients in a small screw-top jar; shake to combine.

SWAP IT Use a drained and rinsed 400g can of lentils instead of cooking green lentils, if preferred.

PREP IT The dressing and salad, without the rocket, can be made up to 2 days in advance and refrigerated in separate airtight containers.

TAKE IT Pack salad (including rocket) and dressing in separate airtight containers. Transport in cooler bags. Refrigerate until ready to serve. Add dressing to salad.

MEAT FREE

Nut Free

Salmon, Barley and Tahini Greens Salad

PREP + COOK TIME 35 MINUTES **SERVES** 2

¾ cup (150g) pearl barley,
  rinsed

1 cup (250ml) vegetable stock

200g green beans, trimmed,
  halved

100g sugar snap peas

1 bunch cavolo nero, stalks
  removed, chopped coarsely

300g wood-roasted or
  hot-smoked salmon pieces

2 tbsp white sesame seeds,
  toasted

TAHINI DRESSING

2 tbsp extra virgin olive oil

1 tbsp tahini

½ tsp finely grated lime rind

1½ tbsp lime juice

2 tsp honey

1 tsp dijon mustard

1 tsp boiling water

1 Place barley, stock and ½ cup (125ml) water in a large heavy-based saucepan with a tight-fitting lid. Bring to the boil over high heat; reduce heat to low. Cook, covered, for 25 minutes or until barley is just tender.

2 Meanwhile, make tahini dressing.

3 Return heat to high; season barley well with salt and add vegetables. Cook, covered, for 3 minutes or until beans and sugar snap peas are just cooked through and cavolo nero wilts. Drain.

4 Combine the barley mixture and salmon pieces; scatter with sesame seeds.

5 Just before serving, spoon dressing over salad.

TAHINI DRESSING Place ingredients in a jug or bowl; whisk until smooth, thick and emulsified. Add more boiling water, if necessary, to achieve the desired consistency. Season to taste. Makes ½ cup.

SWAP IT Substitute kale for the cavolo nero, if you like.

PREP IT Prepare the salad to the end of step 4 the night before or in the morning.

TAKE IT Pack salad and dressing in separate airtight containers. Transport in cooler bags. Refrigerate until ready to serve. Add dressing to salad.

Sesame Chicken Barley Slaw

PREP + COOK TIME *50 MINUTES* **SERVES** *4*

¾ cup (150g) pearl barley
2 chicken breast fillets
1 tbsp extra virgin olive oil
1 tbsp soy sauce
½ tsp sesame oil
½ cup (75g) frozen shelled
   edamame
250g coleslaw salad mix
⅓ cup coriander leaves
2 tsp sesame seeds, toasted

SESAME DRESSING

¼ cup (60ml) rice wine vinegar
2 tbsp extra virgin olive oil
2 tsp soy sauce
½ tsp sesame oil
2 tsp finely grated fresh ginger
1 clove garlic, crushed

1 Place barley and 2¼ cups (560ml) water in a medium saucepan; bring to the boil. Reduce heat to low; cook, covered, for 35 minutes or until tender. Drain; transfer to a large bowl.

2 Meanwhile, preheat oven to 240°C/220°C fan-forced. Line an oven tray with baking paper.

3 Place chicken, olive oil, soy sauce and sesame oil in a large bowl, then season with pepper; toss to coat. Place chicken and marinade on a lined oven tray; roast for 15 minutes or until cooked through. Transfer to a plate; cover loosely with foil. Stand for 5 minutes; slice thinly.

4 Meanwhile, cook edamame in a saucepan of boiling water for 1 minute or until just tender. Drain, then cool in a bowl of cold water; drain again. Add to barley bowl.

5 Make sesame dressing.

6 Add coleslaw mix, coriander, dressing and any tray juices to barley; stir to mix.

7 Top barley salad with chicken; scatter with sesame seeds. Season to taste.

SESAME DRESSING Combine ingredients in a small bowl; season with pepper.

Prep it The recipe can be prepared to the end of step 5 up to 3 days in advance; refrigerate the barley, chicken, edamame and dressing in separate airtight containers. Continue from step 6 the night before or in the morning.

Take it Pack the dressed salad in airtight containers. Transport in cooler bags. Refrigerate until ready to serve.

5
A DAY

CHEAP
EAT

GINGER BEEF and QUINOA SALAD

PREP + COOK TIME 35 MINUTES **SERVES** 2

½ cup (100g) tri-coloured
   quinoa, rinsed well

2 tsp fish sauce

2cm piece fresh ginger,
   grated finely

1 small clove garlic, crushed

¼ tsp freshly ground
   black pepper

200g beef fillet steak

100g sugar snap peas,
   trimmed, halved lengthways

1 baby gem lettuce heart,
   quartered

½ butter lettuce, leaves
   separated

1 trimmed celery stalk, sliced
   thinly on the diagonal

2 green onions, sliced thinly
   lengthways

1 fresh long red chilli, sliced
   thinly (optional)

lime wedges, to serve

LIME & GINGER DRESSING

2 tbsp lime juice

2 tbsp extra virgin olive oil

2cm piece fresh ginger,
   grated finely

1 fresh long red chilli, seeded,
   chopped finely (optional)

1 Place quinoa and 1 cup (250ml) water in a medium saucepan over high heat; bring to the boil. Reduce heat to low; cook, covered, for 12 minutes or until most of the liquid is absorbed. Stand, covered, for 10 minutes. Fluff with a fork.

2 Meanwhile, place fish sauce, ginger, garlic and pepper in a small bowl; stir to combine. Coat beef with ginger mixture. Cook beef in an oiled heavy-based frying pan over high heat, turning, for 4 minutes for medium or until cooked to your liking. Transfer to a plate; cover loosely with foil and stand for 5 minutes. Slice thinly.

3 Meanwhile, boil, steam or microwave sugar snap peas until just tender; drain.

4 Make lime and ginger dressing.

5 Place quinoa, lettuce leaves, celery and peas in a large bowl; toss to combine.

6 Add dressing to salad and toss to combine; top with beef. Scatter with green onion and chilli; serve with lime wedges.

LIME & GINGER DRESSING Place ingredients in a small bowl; stir to combine.

PREP IT Prepare the recipe to the end of step 5 the night before or in the morning.

TAKE IT Pack quinoa mixture, beef, dressing and remaining ingredients in separate airtight containers. Transport in cooler bags. Refrigerate until ready serve. Continue with step 6.

Spicy Roast Salmon Burrito Bowl

PREP + COOK TIME *35 MINUTES* **SERVES** *2*

½ cup (100g) red quinoa, rinsed well

2 x 125g cans kidney beans, drained, rinsed

300g skinless boneless salmon fillet

1½ tsp mexican chilli powder

2 tbsp lime juice

2 tbsp extra virgin olive oil

1 small clove garlic, crushed

60g mixed salad leaves

250g cherry tomatoes, halved

½ small red onion, sliced thinly

1 medium avocado, sliced

2 tbsp coriander leaves and lime wedges, to serve (optional)

1 Preheat oven to 220°C/200°C fan-forced. Line a small oven tray with baking paper.

2 Place quinoa and 1 cup (250ml) water in a small saucepan; bring to the boil. Reduce heat to low; cook, covered, for 20 minutes or until water is absorbed. Remove from heat. Fluff quinoa with a fork; stir through beans.

3 Meanwhile, place salmon on oven tray; sprinkle with chilli powder. Roast salmon for 12 minutes for medium or until cooked to your liking.

4 To make lime dressing, combine lime juice, oil and garlic in a small screw-top jar.

5 Combine quinoa mixture, salad leaves, tomato, onion and avocado.

6 Flake salmon into large pieces; add to salad. Drizzle with lime dressing; season with pepper. Top with coriander and serve with lime wedges.

Prep it Prepare the recipe to the end of step 4 the night before.

Take it Pack salmon, dressing and salad ingredients in separate airtight containers (keep avocado whole). Transport in cooler bags. Refrigerate until ready to serve. Continue from step 5.

5
A DAY

SWAP IT Omit steps 1 and 3 and use purchased wood-roasted or hot-smoked salmon instead of cooking the salmon. Alternatively, try cooked chicken or canned tuna. Use white or tri-coloured quinoa instead of red quinoa. Use sweet paprika or taco seasoning mix instead of mexican chilli powder.

MEAT
FREE

ROASTED VEGETABLE and GRILLED HALOUMI SALAD

PREP + COOK TIME 1 HOUR *SERVES* 4

900g kent pumpkin, skin
   washed, cut into thin wedges
400g mixed baby (dutch)
   carrots, trimmed, scrubbed
¼ cup (60ml) extra virgin
   olive oil
400g broccoli, trimmed,
   cut into small florets
225g haloumi, cut into
   5mm-thick slices
120g mixed salad leaves

OREGANO SALSA
½ cup firmly packed flat-leaf
   parsley leaves, chopped finely
¼ cup firmly packed oregano
   leaves, chopped finely
1 green onion, sliced thinly
1 tbsp baby capers
½ fresh long red chilli, seeded,
   chopped finely
2 tbsp sherry vinegar
¼ cup (60ml) extra virgin
   olive oil

1 Preheat oven to 200°C/180°C fan-forced. Line a large oven tray with baking paper.

2 Place pumpkin and carrots on tray; drizzle with 2 tablespoons of the oil. Season. Roast for 30 minutes; add broccoli to tray. Drizzle broccoli with remaining oil; roast for a further 12 minutes or until vegetables are tender and browned lightly. Cool.

3 Meanwhile, make oregano salsa.

4 Just before serving, heat a baking-paper-lined sandwich press. Cook haloumi for 1 minute or until golden (see tip).

5 Add salad leaves to roast vegetables; drizzle with salsa and season to taste. Top with hot haloumi.

OREGANO SALSA Combine ingredients in a bowl; season to taste. Makes ½ cup.

TIP If serving this at home, pan-fry the haloumi in a non-stick frying pan sprayed with olive oil over medium-high heat for 1 minute on each side or until golden.

SWAP IT Swap haloumi for fetta cubes, if preferred.

PREP IT The recipe can be prepared to the end of step 3 up to 2 days in advance and refrigerated in separate airtight containers. The haloumi can be cooked at home in the morning following the tip above, if preferred.

TAKE IT Pack the roast vegetables, salsa, haloumi and salad leaves in separate airtight containers. Transport in cooler bags. Refrigerate until ready to serve. Continue from step 4.

Shake-it Tuna and Tomato Salad

PREP + COOK TIME 20 MINUTES   **SERVES** 2

2 eggs

2 tbsp extra virgin olive oil

½ tsp finely grated lemon rind

1½ tbsp lemon juice

1 tsp wholegrain mustard

½ tsp caster sugar

2 tsp finely chopped chives

4 cocktail truss tomatoes, sliced

120g yellow grape tomatoes, halved

4 baby cucumbers (qukes), halved lengthways, sliced thickly

2 x 125g cans tuna slices in oil, drained

1 Place eggs in a saucepan of cold water; bring to a simmer. Cook for 5 minutes for soft-boiled, 7 minutes for medium-boiled or 9 minutes for hard-boiled. Cool immediately under cold water. Refrigerate until required.

2 To make dressing, combine oil, rind, lemon juice, mustard, sugar and half the chives in a bowl; mix well. Season to taste.

3 Combine tomato, cucumber and remaining chives in a large bowl. Peel and quarter eggs; add to salad with tuna.

4 Before serving, add dressing to salad. Season to taste.

Swap it   Use regular canned tuna instead of tuna slices, if preferred. Alternatively, swap canned tuna for purchased hot-smoked or wood-roasted salmon pieces, or cook a fresh piece of tuna or salmon instead.

Prep it   Prepare the recipe to the end of step 2 the night before or in the morning.

Take it   Pack salad ingredients, eggs, tuna and dressing in separate airtight containers to assemble at work. Transport in cooler bags. Refrigerate until ready to serve. Continue with step 3.

Gluten Free

Chicken Waldorf Lettuce Cups

PREP + COOK TIME 25 MINUTES (+ COOLING) **SERVES** 4

1 chicken breast fillet
1 red apple, cored, julienned
1 tbsp lemon juice
**1 trimmed celery stalk,
  chopped finely**
**½ cup (50g) walnuts, roasted,
  chopped coarsely**
½ small red onion, sliced thinly
**¼ cup flat-leaf parsley leaves,
  sliced thinly**
150g small red grapes, halved
8 butter lettuce leaves

DRESSING
**¼ cup (75g) whole-egg
  mayonnaise**
1 tbsp lemon juice
2 tsp dijon mustard

1 Place chicken in a small saucepan; cover with water. Bring to a simmer; reduce heat to low-medium. Cook for 7 minutes or until just cooked through; cool in liquid. Drain; shred.

2 Place apple and lemon juice in a medium bowl; toss to combine. Add chicken, celery, walnut, onion, parsley and grapes; stir to combine. Season to taste.

3 Make dressing.

4 Add dressing to chicken mixture; stir to combine. Season.

5 Fill lettuce leaves evenly with chicken mixture.

DRESSING Place ingredients in a small screw-top jar; shake until well combined and emulsified. Season to taste.

SWAP IT Omit step 1, then use the same weight of leftover roast or barbecued chicken, if preferred. Swap the walnuts for sunflower seeds for a nut-free version.

PREP IT Prepare the recipe to the end of step 3 the night before or in the morning.

TAKE IT Pack chicken mixture, dressing and salad leaves in separate airtight containers. Transport in cooler bags. Refrigerate until ready to serve. Continue from step 4.

TROUT, WILD RICE and SNOW PEA SALAD

PREP + COOK TIME 15 MINUTES (+ COOLING) **SERVES** 4

2 x 250g packets microwave
   brown and wild rice
150g snow peas
2 small lebanese cucumbers,
   halved lengthways, sliced
   on the diagonal
2 green onions, sliced thinly
   lengthways
300g portion hot-smoked trout
20g snow pea sprouts

SESAME DRESSING
⅓ cup (80ml) extra virgin
   olive oil
2 tbsp rice wine vinegar
1 tbsp sesame oil
1 tbsp lemon juice
2 tsp honey
2 tsp finely grated fresh ginger
1 tbsp black and white
   sesame seeds

1 Prepare brown and wild rice following packet directions. Transfer to a bowl; cool.

2 Meanwhile, blanch snow peas in a saucepan of boiling water for 1 minute or until tender but still crisp. Drain; slice thickly on the diagonal.

3 Make sesame dressing.

4 Add snow peas, cucumber and green onion to rice; stir gently to mix. Add dressing to salad; stir gently to mix.

5 Add flaked trout and snow pea sprouts to salad; season to taste.

SESAME DRESSING Place ingredients in a small screw-top jar; shake until combined; refrigerate. Makes ¾ cup.

SWAP IT Instead of trout, use purchased hot-smoked or wood-roasted salmon, or leftover cooked chicken or canned tuna, if preferred.

PREP IT Salad and dressing can be made to the end of step 4 the night before or in the morning.

TAKE IT Pack dressed salad, trout and snow pea sprouts in separate airtight containers; refrigerate until ready to take. Transport in cooler bags. Add flaked trout and snow pea sprouts to salad just before serving.

CHICKEN, EGG *and* GREENS SALAD

PREP + COOK TIME 25 MINUTES **SERVES** 2

2 tbsp extra virgin olive oil

1 chicken breast fillet, halved horizontally

2 eggs

100g mixed salad leaves

2 roma tomatoes, chopped

2 slices wholegrain sourdough bread

⅓ cup (100g) caesar dressing

1 Heat oil in a large non-stick frying pan over medium heat. Cook chicken for 4 minutes on each side or until golden and cooked through. Cover loosely with foil; cool. Slice chicken.

2 Meanwhile, place eggs in a saucepan of cold water; bring to a simmer. Cook for 5 minutes for soft-boiled or until cooked to your liking. Cool; peel and quarter.

3 Combine leaves, tomatoes, egg and chicken in a bowl.

4 To make the croutons, toast sourdough in a toaster until crisp and golden. Tear into bite-sized pieces.

5 Before serving, scatter croutons over salad; spoon over dressing. Season to taste.

Swap it Omit step 1 and use leftover cooked chicken or barbecued chicken instead, if preferred.

Prep it Prepare the recipe to the end of step 3 the night before or in the morning.

Take it Pack salad, dressing and bread in separate airtight containers. Transport in cooler bags. Refrigerate until ready to serve. Continue from step 4.

CHEAP EAT

HONEY PUMPKIN *and* FIG SALAD WITH WHIPPED RICOTTA

PREP + COOK TIME 30 MINUTES **SERVES** 2

400g kent pumpkin, diced

¼ cup (60ml) extra virgin
   olive oil

1 tbsp honey

4 small fresh figs, quartered

½ cup (50g) walnuts

160g ricotta

120g baby spinach and rocket
   salad mix

HONEY-MUSTARD DRESSING

⅓ cup (80ml) extra virgin
   olive oil

2 tbsp white balsamic vinegar

2 tsp dijon mustard

1 tsp honey

1 small clove garlic, crushed

1 Preheat oven grill on high. Grease and line an oven tray with baking paper.

2 Place pumpkin, 1 tablespoon of the oil and honey in a bowl; toss to coat. Season to taste. Spread pumpkin mixture over lined tray; grill for 10 minutes or until golden. Add figs to tray; turn in honey and oil mixture. Grill for a further 4 minutes or until figs are caramelised.

3 Meanwhile, make honey-mustard dressing.

4 Using baking paper, lift pumpkin and figs out of tray; cool.

5 Meanwhile, spread walnuts across tray; grill for 2 minutes or until toasted. Cool; chop coarsely.

6 Process ricotta and remaining oil in a small food processor until combined and smooth. Season to taste. Makes ¾ cup.

7 Place pumpkin, figs, walnuts, salad mix and dressing in a bowl; toss gently to combine. Season to taste. Top with spoonfuls of whipped ricotta before serving.

HONEY-MUSTARD DRESSING Place ingredients in a small screw-top jar; shake until combined and emulsified. Season to taste. Makes ½ cup.

Swap it Buy ready-peeled and diced pumpkin, if preferred, or use the same weight of orange sweet potato.

Prep it The pumpkin and figs can be prepared to the end of step 4 up to 2 days in advance. The dressing can be made up to 7 days in advance. The toasted walnuts and whipped ricotta can be made the night before or in the morning.

Take it Pack pumpkin and fig, dressing, walnuts, whipped ricotta and salad leaves in separate airtight containers. Transport in cooler bags. Refrigerate until ready to serve. Continue with step 7.

SWAP IT Use Greek-style yoghurt instead of mayonnaise in the dressing, if preferred.

Green Goodness Salad

2 thick slices soy and linseed
   sourdough bread

1 tbsp olive oil

2 tbsp shelled pistachios,
   chopped coarsely (optional)

2 eggs

100g sugar snap peas

100g snow peas, trimmed

90g broccolini, trimmed,
   sliced lengthways

1 baby cos lettuce, leaves
   separated

1 lebanese cucumber, sliced
   thinly into ribbons

⅔ cup (70g) mixed crunchy
   sprouts

1 avocado, diced

GREEN GOODNESS DRESSING

¼ cup (70g) whole-egg
   mayonnaise

¼ cup (60g) sour cream

1 small clove garlic, crushed

¼ cup coarsely chopped
   flat-leaf parsley

¼ cup coarsely chopped chives

1 tbsp chopped basil

1 tbsp lemon juice

1 Preheat oven to 220°C/200°C fan-forced.

2 Tear bread into chunks; place on an oven tray. Drizzle with oil; toss well to coat. Bake bread for 15 minutes or until crisp and golden. Cool; add pistachios.

3 Meanwhile, place eggs in a small saucepan with enough cold water to just cover. Cover pan with a lid; bring to the boil. Boil eggs for 5 minutes for soft-boiled or continue until cooked to your liking; drain. Cool eggs in a bowl of cold water. Peel and quarter eggs.

4 Cook sugar snap peas, snow peas and broccolini, separately, in a saucepan of boiling water for 2 minutes or until tender but still crisp; drain. Cool in a bowl of cold water; drain. Thinly slice snow peas lengthways; cut sugar snap peas in half.

5 Make green goodness dressing.

6 Divide lettuce, peas, broccolini, cucumber and sprouts among bowls.

7 Top salad with egg, avocado, bread and pistachios. Drizzle with dressing; season to taste.

GREEN GOODNESS DRESSING Blend ingredients in a blender until smooth. Season to taste. Makes ¾ cup.

Prep it   Salad and dressing can be made to the end of step 6 the night before or in the morning.

Take it   Pack the greens, egg, bread and pistachio mixture, dressing and whole avocado in separate airtight containers. Transport in cooler bags. Refrigerate until ready to serve. Continue with step 7. You can also omit steps 1 and 2 and toast the bread in a toaster at work, then tear into chunks just before serving.

5 A DAY

Salmon, Sugar Snap Pea and Pearl Couscous Salad

PREP + COOK TIME 25 MINUTES **SERVES** 2

1 lemon, sliced thinly crossways

250g skinless boneless
   salmon fillet

¼ cup (60ml) extra virgin
   olive oil

1 cup (150g) frozen broad beans

100g sugar snap peas

¾ cup (150g) pearl couscous

1 green onion, sliced thinly
   lengthways

¼ cup flat-leaf parsley leaves

¼ cup dill leaves

1 tbsp lemon juice

AVOCADO DRESSING

½ medium avocado

2 tbsp japanese mayonnaise

2 tbsp lemon juice

1 Preheat oven to 200°C/180°C fan-forced. Grease and line an oven tray with baking paper.

2 Arrange lemon slices in the approximate shape of salmon fillet on centre of tray. Season salmon with salt and pepper on both sides; place on top of lemon. Drizzle with 1 tablespoon of the oil; roast for 10 minutes or until just cooked through. Cover loosely with foil; stand.

3 Meanwhile, blanch broad beans in a saucepan of simmering water for 2 minutes or until tender. Remove using a slotted spoon; refresh in iced water. In same pan, blanch sugar snap peas for 1 minute or until bright green and tender. Drain; refresh in iced water. Pod broad beans; set aside.

4 Bring a clean saucepan of water to the boil; cook pearl couscous for 6 minutes or until tender. Rinse under cold water; drain. Transfer couscous to a bowl; add broad beans, sugar snap peas, green onion, herbs, remaining oil and lemon juice.

5 Flake salmon into large chunks.

6 Make avocado dressing.

7 Gently toss couscous mixture and salmon together; spoon over avocado dressing. Season to taste.

AVOCADO DRESSING Process ingredients with 2 tablespoons water in a small food processor until smooth; season to taste. Makes ¾ cup.

PREP IT Prepare the salad to the end of step 6 the night before or in the morning.

TAKE IT Pack couscous mixture, flaked salmon and dressing in separate airtight containers. Transport in cooler bags. Refrigerate until ready to serve. Continue with step 7.

Nut Free

SWAP IT Omit roasting the salmon fillet and use purchased wood-roasted or hot-smoked salmon, or canned tuna instead. Use regular mayonnaise instead of japanese mayonnaise, if preferred.

Sesame Chicken Katsu Salad

PREP + COOK TIME 25 MINUTES **SERVES** 2

1 cup (200g) frozen shelled
  edamame
4 chicken tenderloins
¼ cup (40g) plain flour
1 egg, beaten lightly
½ cup (40g) panko
  breadcrumbs
2 tbsp white sesame seeds
½ cup (125ml) oil,
  for shallow-frying
60g snow pea tendrils
2 baby cucumbers (qukes),
  sliced on the diagonal
2 green onions, sliced thinly
  lengthways

DRESSING
⅓ cup (100g) japanese
  mayonnaise
2 tbsp rice wine vinegar
½ tsp shichimi togarashi

1 Cook edamame in a small saucepan of boiling water until tender; drain. Rinse under cold water; drain again.

2 To make the chicken katsu, lightly dust chicken in flour, shaking off any excess. Coat in egg, then crumbs combined with sesame seeds.

3 Place oil in a small heavy-based frying pan until a third full. Heat over medium-high heat until hot; cook chicken for 4 minutes on each side or until golden and cooked through. Drain on paper towel. Cool; slice thickly.

4 Make dressing.

5 Divide chicken, snow pea tendrils, cucumber, edamame and green onion between bowls; season to taste.

6 Before serving, drizzle salad with dressing.

DRESSING Combine ingredients in a small bowl. Makes ½ cup.

Swap it   Use regular mayonnaise instead of japanese mayonnaise, if you like.

Prep it   Prepare the salad to the end of step 4 the night before or in the morning.

Take it   Pack the chicken, greens and dressing in separate airtight containers. Transport in cooler bags. Refrigerate until ready to serve. Continue from step 5. Chicken can be warmed in a microwave, if you like.

CHICKEN and BROAD BEAN PESTO SALAD

PREP + COOK TIME *35 MINUTES* **SERVES** *4*

2 chicken breast fillets, halved horizontally

½ cup (125ml) extra virgin olive oil

2 tsp finely chopped rosemary

¼ tsp chilli flakes (optional)

300g frozen broad beans, shelled

1 small clove garlic, crushed

1 tbsp pine nuts

⅓ cup (25g) finely grated parmesan

½ tsp finely grated lemon rind

1½ tbsp lemon juice

120g baby spinach leaves

1 bunch red radishes, trimmed, halved, quartered or sliced

250g cherry tomatoes, halved

1 Preheat a chargrill plate (or pan) on high heat.

2 Place chicken, 2 tablespoons of the oil, rosemary and chilli flakes in a bowl; mix to coat. Season chicken; grill for 4 minutes on each side or until cooked through. Cool; slice thickly or shred.

3 Cook broad beans in a saucepan of boiling water for 2 minutes or until tender; drain. Plunge into iced cold water; drain again.

4 To make the pesto, process ½ cup of the broad beans, remaining oil, the garlic, pine nuts, parmesan, lemon rind and juice until a smooth paste forms; season to taste. Stir in 1 tablespoon water to thin. Refrigerate until required.

5 Divide spinach, radish, tomato, remaining broad beans and chicken among bowls.

6 Just before serving, top salad with spoonfuls of pesto. Season to taste with pepper.

PREP IT The chicken can be cooked following the instructions in steps 1 and 2 up to 2 days ahead and refrigerated in an airtight container. The pesto can be made up to 3 days ahead and refrigerated in an airtight container. Prepare the recipe to the end of step 5 the night before or in the morning.

TAKE IT Pack chicken salad and pesto in separate airtight containers. Transport in cooler bags. Refrigerate until ready to serve. Continue with step 6.

CHEAP EAT

SWAP IT Omit cooking the chicken and use barbecued chicken, or try purchased wood-roasted or hot-smoked salmon pieces instead. To make this nut-free, swap the pine nuts in the pesto with 2 tablespoons sunflower seeds.

POKE BOWL

PREP + COOK TIME *20 MINUTES* **SERVES** *2*

1 x 250g packet microwave
   brown rice
2 tbsp tamari
2 tsp rice wine vinegar
½ tsp sesame oil
150g smoked salmon slices
1 avocado, diced
50g japanese seaweed salad
   (see tip)
1 small lebanese cucumber,
   halved lengthways,
   seeded, sliced
2 radishes, trimmed,
   sliced thinly
2 green onions, sliced thinly
   lengthways
toasted white sesame seeds,
   to serve (optional)

1 Cook rice following packet directions.

2 Meanwhile, whisk tamari, vinegar and sesame oil in a medium jug. Add 2 tablespoons of the tamari dressing to warm rice; stir to combine.

3 Top rice with salmon, avocado, seaweed salad, cucumber and radish. Scatter with green onion and sesame seeds. Serve with remaining dressing drizzled on top, or to the side for dipping.

TIP   Seaweed salad is available from fishmongers, sushi bars, some major supermarkets and salad bars.

SWAP IT   Swap the seaweed salad for edamame pods, if preferred.

PREP IT   The recipe can be prepared to the end of step 2 the night before or in the morning. The cucumber, radish and green onion can also be prepared the night before or in the morning.

TAKE IT   Pack the rice mixture, salmon, seaweed salad and vegetables in separate airtight containers. Transport in cooler bags. Refrigerate until ready to serve. Continue with step 3.

Gluten Free

Mushroom Arancini

PREP + COOK TIME 1 HOUR 25 MINUTES (+ STANDING & FREEZING) **MAKES** 28

3 cups (750ml) salt-reduced
vegetable stock

25g dried shiitake mushrooms

250g mushrooms

2 tbsp olive oil

30g butter

1 small onion, chopped finely

2 cloves garlic, crushed

½ cup (100g) arborio rice

⅓ cup (80ml) white wine

½ cup (40g) grated parmesan

1 cup (150g) plain flour,
seasoned

3 eggs, beaten lightly

1½ cups (115g) panko
breadcrumbs

2 tbsp thyme leaves,
chopped finely

14 cherry bocconcini (220g),
halved

oil, for deep-frying

extra thyme sprigs (optional)
and lemon wedges, to serve

1 Place stock and dried mushrooms in a large saucepan over high heat. Bring to the boil; reduce heat to low and simmer for 8 minutes. Stand, covered, for 20 minutes to infuse; drain, reserving liquid and mushrooms. Cover to keep warm.

2 Meanwhile, process dried and fresh mushrooms separately, using the pulse function, until chopped finely; transfer to separate bowls.

3 Heat olive oil in a large deep heavy-based frying pan over high heat. Cook fresh mushroom for 6 minutes or until liquid is evaporated and mushroom is golden. Transfer to a bowl.

4 Add butter to same frying pan over medium heat. Cook onion, stirring, for 4 minutes or until golden. Add garlic; cook for 1 minute. Add rice; cook, stirring, for 2 minutes. Increase heat to high and add wine; cook, stirring, until wine is absorbed.

5 Add one-third of the mushroom broth; cook, stirring, for 7 minutes or until almost absorbed. Repeat with remaining broth in two batches. The rice will take approximately 20 minutes in total to cook. Stir through chopped dried and fresh mushrooms and half the parmesan; season to taste.

6 Transfer risotto to a large shallow roasting pan; freeze for 20 minutes or until chilled and firm.

7 Place seasoned flour, beaten egg, and combined panko, thyme leaves and remaining parmesan in separate shallow bowls. Roll 1 tablespoon portions of risotto into 28 balls. Push half a piece of bocconcini into centre of each risotto ball, then coat in flour, egg and breadcrumb mixture.

8 Heat oil for deep-frying in a deep heavy-based saucepan to 170°C. Cook arancini, in batches, for 4 minutes or until crisp, golden and bocconcini is melted. Drain on paper towel.

9 Sprinkle with extra thyme sprigs; serve with lemon wedges.

Prep It Arancini can be made up to 3 days in advance and refrigerated in an airtight container. They can also be frozen for up to 2 months; thaw in the fridge before reheating.

Take It Pack in airtight containers. Transport in cooler bags. Refrigerate until ready to serve. Reheat in a microwave.

SERVE IT Serve arancini with a purchased lemon aïoli or combine ⅓ cup whole-egg mayonnaise with the finely grated zest and juice of 1 medium lemon. Season to taste.

SERVE IT Karaage chicken can also be tossed through noodle salads or served in bao buns with sriracha mayo and an Asian-style slaw.

KARAAGE CHICKEN WITH SRIRACHA MAYO

PREP + COOK TIME 30 MINUTES (+ REFRIGERATION) *SERVES* 4

1 tbsp finely grated fresh ginger

2 cloves garlic, crushed

2 tbsp tamari

1 tbsp mirin

1 tsp sesame oil

600g chicken thigh fillets,
   cut into bite-sized pieces

oil, for deep-frying

2 cups (300g) potato flour

⅓ cup (100g) japanese
   mayonnaise

1 tbsp sriracha sauce (optional)

1 Place ginger, garlic, tamari, mirin and sesame oil in a large bowl; whisk to combine. Add chicken; turn to coat in marinade. Cover; refrigerate for at least 1 hour, turning occasionally.

2 Heat oil for deep-frying in a deep heavy-based frying pan to 170°C.

3 Place potato flour in a shallow bowl. Drain chicken well; discard excess marinade. Add chicken pieces, in batches, to flour; toss to coat, shaking off excess.

4 Cook chicken, in batches, for 4 minutes or until crisp and golden on the outside and chicken is cooked through. Drain on paper towel. Increase oil to 180°C. Cook in batches a second time for 1 minute.

5 Combine mayonnaise and sriracha in a small bowl. Serve chicken karaage with sriracha mayonnaise.

Swap it Use your favourite mayonnaise instead of japanese mayonnaise, if preferred. Alternatively, instead of making sriracha mayonnaise, serve with your favourite purchased aïoli.

Prep it Karaage chicken and sriracha mayo can be made the night before.

Take it Pack cooled chicken and sriracha mayonnaise in separate airtight containers. Transport in cooler bags. Refrigerate until ready to take. You can eat the chicken cold or reheat it in a microwave, if preferred.

Gluten Free

Pork and Apple Sausage Rolls

PREP + COOK TIME 55 MINUTES (+ REFRIGERATION) **MAKES** 36

2 shallots, chopped coarsely

1 medium fennel bulb,
  chopped coarsely

2 tbsp olive oil

2 medium green apples,
  cored, grated

1 medium carrot, grated

4 cloves garlic, chopped finely

1kg minced pork

⅓ cup finely chopped fresh
  flat-leaf parsley

2 tbsp thyme leaves, chopped

6 sheets frozen puff pastry,
  thawed

2 eggs, beaten lightly

3 tsp white sesame seeds

1 Preheat oven to 200°C/180°C fan-forced. Grease and line two large oven trays with baking paper.

2 Process shallot and fennel in a food processor, using the pulse button, until chopped finely.

3 Heat oil in a large heavy-based frying pan over medium heat. Cook shallot and fennel for 4 minutes or until golden. Place apple in a colander; squeeze out all the excess liquid. Add apple, carrot and garlic to pan; cook for 2 minutes. Transfer to a sieve; press down to remove excess liquid.

4 Place pork mince, parsley, thyme and cooled vegetable mixture in a large bowl; season. Using clean hands, mix ingredients until well combined.

5 Cut pastry sheets in half lengthways. Spoon ⅓ cup of the mince mixture lengthways along centre of each pastry piece. Turn one long side of pastry over mince mixture. Brush pastry flap with a little of the egg. Turn over other long side of pastry to enclose mince mixture. Refrigerate for 30 minutes.

6 Cut each roll into thirds using a small sharp knife. Make two shallow cuts in the top of each sausage roll to allow steam to escape during baking. Place rolls, seam-side down, on trays; brush rolls with egg and scatter with sesame seeds.

7 Bake sausage rolls for 30 minutes or until pastry is puffed and golden and pork mixture is cooked through. Transfer to wire racks to cool, if not serving straight away.

PREP IT Sausage rolls can be made up to 3 days in advance and refrigerated in a paper-towel-lined airtight container. They will also freeze for up to 3 months; thaw in the fridge before reheating.

TAKE IT Pack sausage rolls in airtight containers. Transport in cooler bags. Refrigerate until ready to serve. Reheat in a microwave or eat at room temperature.

CHEAP EAT

SWAP IT To make this gluten-free, use gluten-free puff pastry sheets. Swap sesame seeds for fennel seeds, if you like.

SERVE IT Serve with tomato sauce or relish.

Beetroot and Fetta Whip

PREP TIME 10 MINUTES   **MAKES** 3 CUPS

180g marinated persian
   fetta in oil
500g vacuum-packed cooked
   beetroot, drained, patted dry
⅓ cup (35g) walnuts, toasted
¼ cup firmly packed mint leaves
1 tsp finely grated lemon rind
¼ cup (60ml) lemon juice
1 tsp cumin seeds, toasted
   (see tip)

1 Drain fetta in a sieve over a measuring jug, reserving
⅓ cup (80ml) oil.
2 Process or blend ingredients, including reserved oil,
until almost smooth; season to taste with salt and pepper.

TIP   To toast seeds, cook in a small frying pan over medium
heat, shaking pan gently, until fragrant.

SWAP IT   To make this nut-free, use sunflower seeds
instead of walnuts.

PREP IT   Dip can be made up to 3 days in advance and
refrigerated in an airtight container.

TAKE IT   Pack dip in serving-sized airtight containers.
Transport in cooler bags. Refrigerate until ready to serve.

SERVE IT   Serve dip with crispbread or crudites.

MEAT FREE

TWISTED SCROLLS

PREP + COOK TIME 40 MINUTES   **MAKES 9 PER VARIATION**

For the basic dough, preheat oven to 200°C/180°C fan-forced. Grease and line a 20cm square cake pan with baking paper. Sift 2 cups self-raising flour, ½ tsp bicarbonate of soda and 1 tsp salt into a bowl; rub in 50g chopped chilled butter with your fingertips. Add approximately 1 cup buttermilk and mix to a soft, sticky dough. Turn dough onto a floured surface; knead lightly until smooth. Roll into a 30cm x 40cm rectangle.

CHEESYMITE SCROLLS

Make basic dough above. Warm 1½ tbsp Vegemite in a microwave to soften; spread over dough. Scatter with ½ cup grated tasty cheese. Roll dough tightly from long side. Using a serrated knife, trim the ends; cut roll into nine slices. Place scrolls, cut-side up, in pan; scatter scrolls with another ½ cup cheese. Bake scrolls for 25 minutes or until cooked through. Cool in pan.

PIZZA SCROLLS

Make basic dough above. Spread dough with ⅓ cup pizza sauce. Scatter with 150g coarsely chopped ham, ½ cup well-drained, dried and coarsely chopped canned pineapple and ½ cup grated pizza cheese. Roll dough tightly from long side. Using a serrated knife, trim the ends; cut roll into nine slices. Place scrolls, cut-side up, in pan; scatter scrolls with another ½ cup cheese. Bake scrolls for 25 minutes or until cooked through. Cool in pan.

APPLE and CINNAMON SCROLLS

Make basic dough above. Combine 2 coarsely grated apples, 2 tbsp brown sugar and ½ tsp ground cinnamon in a bowl. Scatter apple mixture over dough. Roll dough tightly from long side. Using a serrated knife, trim ends; cut roll into nine slices. Place scrolls, cut-side up, in pan; brush with 1 tsp milk. Bake scrolls for 25 minutes or until cooked through. Cool in pan.

BLUEBERRY and CHIA SEED SCROLLS

Make basic dough above. Combine 125g fresh blueberries, 1 tbsp caster sugar, 1 tbsp chia seeds and 1 tsp finely grated orange rind in a bowl. Scatter berry mixture over dough. Roll dough tightly from long side. Using a serrated knife, trim the ends; cut roll into nine slices. Place scrolls, cut-side up, in pan; brush with 1 tsp milk and sprinkle with 1 tbsp demerara sugar. Bake scrolls for 25 minutes or until cooked through. Cool in pan.

Moroccan Dip

PREP + COOK TIME 25 MINUTES (+ COOLING) **MAKES** 3½ CUPS

1 tbsp extra virgin olive oil

5 green onions, chopped

1 clove garlic, crushed

1 tbsp finely chopped
    coriander stems

2 tsp ras el hanout

1 tsp harissa paste

4 medium carrots, grated
    coarsely (see tip)

1 small orange sweet potato,
    grated coarsely (see tip)

½ cup (125ml) vegetable or
    chicken stock

400g can cannellini beans,
    drained, rinsed

1 Heat oil in a large heavy-based saucepan over medium-high heat; cook onion, garlic, coriander and ras el hanout for 1 minute. Add harissa, carrot and sweet potato; cook, stirring, for 2 minutes. Add stock and bring to the boil; reduce heat to low. Cook, covered, for 5 minutes or until vegetables soften.

2 Transfer vegetable mixture to a food processor and add beans; process until smooth. Season to taste. Leave to cool.

TIP You will need about 500g carrots and 250g sweet potato for this recipe.

PREP IT Dip can be made up to 3 days in advance and refrigerated in an airtight container.

TAKE IT Pack dip in serving-sized airtight containers. Transport in cooler bags. Refrigerate until ready to serve.

SERVE IT Serve dip with lebanese bread, crisp pitta chips or your choice of raw vegetables, such as trimmed snow peas, sugar snap peas, baby cucumbers, celery sticks and sliced capsicum.

TAHINI-DATE YOGHURT CUPS

PREP TIME 15 MINUTES **MAKES** 1 CUP

1 cup (230g) fresh dates, pitted

⅓ cup (90g) hulled tahini

2 tsp sesame seeds

2 tsp linseeds

1 tsp poppy seeds

⅛ tsp sea salt flakes

125g Greek-style yoghurt,
  per serve

mixed berries, to serve

SWEET DUKKAH

1½ tbsp unsalted hazelnuts

1½ tbsp pistachios

1 tbsp white sesame seeds

3 tsp coriander seeds

1 tbsp brown sugar

¾ tsp ground cinnamon

¾ tsp ground cardamom

1 To make the tahini-date spread, place dates in a small heatproof bowl. Cover with boiling water; stand for 5 minutes. Drain, reserving 2 tablespoons liquid. Blend or process dates with reserved liquid, tahini, seeds and salt until smooth.

2 Spoon tahini-date spread into a 1-cup (250ml) capacity jar; refrigerate while preparing sweet dukkah.

3 Make sweet dukkah.

4 Just before serving, spoon yoghurt into a cup, bowl, jar or glass. Swirl in tahini-date spread to taste. Top with berries; sprinkle with sweet dukkah.

SWEET DUKKAH Preheat oven to 200°C/180°C fan-forced. Place nuts and seeds on an oven tray lined with baking paper; roast for 5 minutes. Crush coarsely with a mortar and pestle; cool. Combine sugar, spices and nut mixture in a small bowl; mix well. Makes ½ cup.

Tip For a chocolate spread, blend in 1 tablespoon cacao powder with the ingredients in step 1.

Swap it To make this nut-free, use ¼ cup natural seed mix (pepitas and sunflower seeds) instead of the hazelnuts and pistachios in the dukkah.

Prep it Tahini-date spread can be made up to 4 weeks in advance and refrigerated in a screw-top jar. Sweet dukkah can be made up to 2 weeks in advance and stored in an airtight container.

Take it Pack spread, dukkah, yoghurt and berries in separate airtight containers. Transport in cooler bags. Refrigerate until ready to serve.

Gluten Free

SERVE IT Leftover tahini-date spread can be spread over pancakes or toast in place of jam, or stirred into a banana smoothie.

Gluten Free

James

Kate

Mini Pancetta and Rice Frittatas

PREP + COOK TIME 1 HOUR 10 MINUTES **MAKES** 12

½ cup (75g) frozen broad beans

2 cups (500ml) chicken stock

40g butter

1 small onion, chopped finely

1 cup (200g) arborio rice

½ tsp finely grated lemon rind

2 eggs, beaten lightly

2 tbsp finely chopped
   flat-leaf parsley

¾ cup (60g) grated parmesan

12 slices pancetta

1 Preheat oven to 180°C/160°C fan-forced. Grease a 12-hole (⅓-cup/80ml) muffin pan.

2 Cook broad beans in a saucepan of simmering water for 2 minutes or until tender but still green. Refresh in iced water, then drain; peel.

3 Place stock in a medium saucepan; bring to a simmer.

4 Meanwhile, melt butter in a large heavy-based saucepan over medium heat; cook onion, stirring, for 5 minutes or until softened. Add rice, stirring to coat grains.

5 Add ½ cup (125ml) of the stock to pan of rice; reduce heat to low. Cook, stirring, for 2 minutes or until stock is absorbed. Continue stirring and adding ½ cup (125ml) stock at a time for about 25 minutes or until rice is creamy and tender. Stir in beans, rind, egg, parsley and ½ cup of the parmesan. Season with freshly ground pepper.

6 Place a pancetta slice in each muffin hole, covering base and side of each hole. Divide rice mixture evenly among pan holes; scatter with remaining parmesan. Bake for 25 minutes or until frittatas are golden and set. Stand in pan for 5 minutes; transfer to a wire rack to cool.

Swap it Use peas, chopped asparagus or peeled edamame instead of broad beans, if preferred.

Prep it Frittatas can be made up to 3 days in advance and refrigerated in an airtight container. Or wrap individual frittatas in plastic wrap and freeze for up to 1 month; thaw in the fridge before reheating.

Take it Pack frittatas in separate airtight containers. Transport in cooler bags. Refrigerate until ready to serve. Reheat in a microwave, if you like.

CRAISIN TOAST

PREP + COOK TIME 45 MINUTES (+ STANDING & COOLING) **SERVES** 12

300ml warmed milk

1 x 7g sachet dry yeast

¼ cup (55g) light brown sugar

1½ tsp fine salt

3 cups (450g) plain flour

1 tsp mixed spice

1 tsp ground cinnamon

1⅓ cups (200g) dried
   sweetened cranberries

1 Mix ¼ cup of the warmed milk, the yeast, 1 teaspoon of the sugar and the salt in a small bowl. Stand in a warm place for 10 minutes or until mixture is frothy.

2 Sift flour, remaining sugar and spices into a large bowl. Add yeast mixture and remaining warmed milk; mix until a dough forms.

3 Turn dough out onto a floured work surface; knead for 10 minutes or until smooth and elastic. Place in an oiled large bowl; cover with a clean tea towel. Stand in a warm place for 1 hour or until doubled in size.

4 Preheat oven to 180°C/160°C fan-forced. Lightly grease a 10cm x 21cm (base measurement), 6½cm deep loaf pan; line base and sides with baking paper, extending paper 5cm over long sides.

5 Punch dough down in bowl, then turn out onto a floured surface. Knead in cranberries. Shape into a log; place in prepared pan. Cover with a clean tea towel; stand in a warm place for 30 minutes or until doubled in size.

6 Bake for 30 minutes or until loaf is golden and sounds hollow when tapped on top. Transfer to a wire rack.

PREP IT Craisin loaf can be made up to 3 days in advance; keep wrapped in plastic wrap, then foil, in an airtight container. Or cut the loaf into slices and wrap individually in plastic wrap, then freeze for up to 1 month.

SERVE IT Cut into slices and eat fresh or toasted with butter. Sprinkle toast with cinnamon sugar before serving, if you like.

CHEAP
EAT

Loaded Hummus

Pomegranate and Pine Nut Hummus

PREP TIME 10 MINUTES
SERVES 4

Stir 1 tsp ground cumin into a 200g tub of hummus. Top with toasted pine nuts, pomegranate seeds and a little thinly sliced red onion; season to taste. Drizzle with extra virgin olive oil.

Seed and Spice Hummus

PREP + COOK TIME 5 MINUTES
SERVES 4

Heat 2 tbsp olive oil in a small frying pan over medium heat; cook 2 tbsp pepitas and 1 tsp each cumin seeds, sesame seeds and crushed coriander seeds, stirring, until toasted. Scatter over a 200g tub of hummus; season to taste. Top with thin strips of lemon rind; drizzle with extra virgin olive oil.

Hummus with Harissa Chickpeas

PREP + COOK TIME 25 MINUTES
SERVES 4

Pat a drained and rinsed 400g can chickpeas dry with paper towel; place in a bowl. Add 1 tbsp each harissa and olive oil; stir. Spread chickpea mixture, in a single layer, on a baking-paper-lined oven tray. Bake in a 200°C/180°C fan-forced oven, stirring three times during cooking, for 20 minutes or until well browned and slightly crunchy. Scatter over a 200g tub of hummus; top with small mint leaves; season to taste. Drizzle with extra virgin olive oil.

Greek Salad Hummus

PREP TIME 10 MINUTES
SERVES 4

Top a 200g tub of hummus with finely diced cucumber, ripe tomato and red onion, crumbled fetta and chopped pitted kalamata olives. Sprinkle with dried Greek-style oregano; season to taste. Drizzle with extra virgin olive oil.

Apricot, orange blossom and Coconut squares

PREP TIME 15 MINUTES (+ REFRIGERATION)   **MAKES** 24

400g dried apricots

2 cups (160g) desiccated coconut

2 cups (320g) unsalted roasted cashews

1 cup (120g) almond meal

½ cup (40g) quinoa flakes

2 tbsp white chia seeds

¼ cup (70g) coconut yoghurt

2 tbsp orange blossom water

2 tbsp lemon juice

2 tbsp honey

½ cup (35g) shaved coconut, toasted (optional)

1 Line a 16cm x 25cm (base measurement), 2cm deep slice pan with baking paper, extending paper 5cm over long sides.

2 Process all ingredients, except toasted shaved coconut, until finely chopped and combined; mixture should clump together and start to come away from side of processor bowl.

3 Press apricot mixture into prepared pan, using the back of a large spoon to spread evenly; scatter top with toasted coconut. Cover with plastic wrap; refrigerate for 1 hour to firm.

4 Transfer slice to a chopping board; cut into 24 squares.

Swap it   You can use oat flakes instead of quinoa flakes, if you like.

Prep it   Slice can be made up to 2 weeks in advance and refrigerated in an airtight container.

Gluten Free

TWISTED ZUCCHINI SLICE

PREP + COOK TIME 1 HOUR 10 MINUTES (+ COOLING) **MAKES 8**

1 cup (220g) risoni
500g zucchini, grated coarsely
(see tip)
½ tsp finely grated lemon rind
250g haloumi, grated coarsely
4 green onions, chopped finely
1 clove garlic, crushed
⅓ cup (25g) finely grated
parmesan
2 tbsp finely chopped
flat-leaf parsley
4 eggs, beaten lightly
½ cup (75g) self-raising flour

1 Cook risoni in a saucepan of boiling salted water for 8 minutes or until just tender. Drain; cool.

2 Preheat oven to 180°C/160°C fan-forced. Grease a 20cm x 30cm slice pan; line with baking paper, extending paper 5cm over long sides.

3 Squeeze as much liquid from zucchini as possible; transfer to a large bowl. Add pasta, rind, half the haloumi, the green onion, garlic, parmesan, parsley and egg; stir to combine. Add flour; stir well to combine. Season.

4 Pour mixture into prepared pan, smoothing surface; scatter with remaining haloumi. Bake for 45 minutes or until firm, golden and cooked through. Cool in pan for 15 minutes. Cut into eight pieces.

TIP You will need about 4 medium zucchini for this recipe.

PREP IT Zucchini slice can be made up to 2 days in advance; refrigerate portion-sized pieces in baking paper, then plastic wrap, in an airtight container. Or freeze individual pieces between baking paper in an airtight container for up to 2 months. For school lunch boxes, cut into 16 smaller slices.

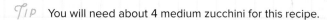

TAKE IT Pack individual slices in airtight containers. Transport in cooler bags. Refrigerate until ready to serve. Reheat in a microwave, if you like.

MEAT FREE

MINI MUESLI CUPS

PREP + COOK TIME 20 MINUTES (+ REFRIGERATION) **MAKES** 12

1½ cups (135g) rolled oats
1 cup (50g) dried flaked
   coconut
⅔ cup (110g) sultanas
⅔ cup (90g) dried sweetened
   cranberries
¼ cup (50g) pepitas
¼ cup (35g) sunflower seeds
75g butter
¼ tsp sea salt flakes
½ cup (175g) honey
1 tsp vanilla extract

1 Grease a 12-hole (⅓-cup/80ml) muffin pan. Cut 24 strips of baking paper; line each hole with two baking paper strips, forming a cross pattern; alternatively, use cupcake cases.
2 Stir oats and coconut in a medium non-stick frying pan over medium heat for 3 minutes or until lightly toasted.
3 Combine sultanas, cranberries and both seeds in a measuring jug.
4 Pulse ¾ cup toasted oat mixture and half the fruit and seed mixture in a food processor until finely chopped; stir into the remaining oat mixture with the remaining fruit and seed mixture.
5 Place butter, salt, honey and vanilla in a medium frying pan; stir over medium heat until butter melts and mixture bubbles. Add combined dry mixtures; stir for 2 minutes or until mixture is well combined and sticky.
6 Spoon mixture into pan holes, pressing lightly to level surface. Refrigerate for 10 minutes to chill; repeat pressing. Refrigerate for at least 1 hour to firm. Use baking paper to remove muesli cups from pan holes.

Swap it   If nut allergies aren't an issue, instead of using sultanas, cranberries and the seeds, use two 150g packets of a snacking mix containing roasted almonds, peanuts, hazelnuts, dried sweetened cranberries, pepitas and sunflower seeds. Alternatively, use any combination of chopped nuts and seeds, weight for weight, for the dried fruits, coconut and seeds, or 4⅓ cups of your favourite muesli.

Prep it   Muesli cups can be made up to 1 week in advance and refrigerated in an airtight container.

TIP To make oat bars instead of cups, press mixture into a greased and baking-paper-lined 18cm square cake pan. Refrigerate and press as directed in step 6, then cut into bars.

ROAST CAULIFLOWER HUMMUS

PREP + COOK TIME 35 MINUTES (+ COOLING) **MAKES** 3 CUPS

**1 small cauliflower (1kg),
cut into florets**
**⅓ cup (80ml) extra virgin
olive oil**
3 cloves garlic, unpeeled
400g can chickpeas
⅓ cup (95g) cashew spread
¼ cup (60ml) lemon juice

1 Preheat oven to 200°C/180°C fan-forced. Line a large oven tray with baking paper.
2 Place cauliflower, 1 tablespoon of the oil and the garlic in a large bowl; stir to coat, then season. Arrange cauliflower and garlic, in a single layer, on lined tray; roast for 25 minutes or until tender. Cool to room temperature; peel garlic.
3 Drain chickpeas in a sieve over a measuring jug, reserving ⅓ cup liquid. Rinse chickpeas under cold water; drain.
4 Process cooled cauliflower, garlic, chickpeas, reserved liquid, cashew spread and lemon juice until smooth. With motor operating, add remaining oil in a steady stream; process until combined. Season to taste.

SWAP IT To make this nut-free, use tahini instead of cashew spread.

PREP IT Dip can be made up to 3 days in advance and refrigerated in an airtight container; cover surface with a thin layer of extra virgin olive oil to prevent it from drying out. This recipe is not suitable to freeze.

TAKE IT Pack dip in serving-sized airtight containers. Transport in cooler bags. Refrigerate until ready to serve.

SERVE IT 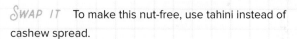 Serve dip with your choice of raw vegetables, such as peeled baby carrots, trimmed asparagus spears and green beans. Sprinkle with toasted dukkah.

CHEAP EAT

CHOCOLATE BUBBLE SLICE

PREP + COOK TIME 20 MINUTES (+ OVERNIGHT REFRIGERATION) **MAKES** 16

200g condensed milk

¼ cup (70g) hulled tahini,
   at room temperature (see tip)

10 pitted medjool dates (200g),
   chopped coarsely

1 tsp ground cinnamon

¼ cup (50g) pepitas

¼ cup (35g) sunflower seeds

2 tbsp black sesame seeds

¼ cup (30g) sweetened
   cranberries

⅔ cup (18g) puffed quinoa

100g dark chocolate, melted

10g butter, melted

1 Grease an 18cm x 27cm slice pan; line with baking paper, extending paper 5cm over long sides.

2 Cook condensed milk, tahini and dates in a medium heavy-based saucepan over medium heat, stirring, for 3 minutes or until melted and combined. Transfer to a large heatproof bowl; stir in cinnamon, seeds, cranberries and quinoa. Press mixture into pan.

3 Combine melted chocolate and butter; drizzle over slice. Refrigerate overnight or until firm. Cut into 16 pieces.

TIP Use only the thick, non-oily part of the tahini to keep the base firm.

SWAP IT Puffed quinoa is available from health food stores; you can substitute with puffed rice, if you like. If nut allergies are not an issue, use ½ cup (140g) crunchy peanut butter and 2 tablespoons coconut oil instead of the condensed milk.

PREP IT Slice can be made up to 1 week in advance and refrigerated in an airtight container.

NUT FREE

CHEAP
EAT

Loaded Fetta Muffins

PREP + COOK TIME 45 MINUTES   MAKES 12 PER VARIATION

Baby Spinach and FETTA

Heat 2 tbsp olive oil in a frying pan; cook 1 finely chopped small onion, stirring, for 2 minutes or until softened. Add 100g baby spinach leaves; cook, stirring, for 1 minute or until wilted. Cool. Add to green onion and fetta base muffin mixture below when adding the fetta. Continue with recipe.

Sweet Potato and FETTA

Steam, boil or microwave 1 small orange sweet potato (175g) cut into 1cm dice; cool. Add to green onion and fetta base muffin mixture below left when adding the fetta, along with and 1 tbsp thyme leaves; mix gently to combine (do not over-mix; mixture should be lumpy). Spoon mixture into pan holes. Scatter with 2 tbsp pepitas. Continue with recipe.

Green Onion and FETTA BASE

Preheat oven to 200°C/180°C fan-forced. Grease a 12-hole (⅓-cup) muffin pan. Sift 2 cups self-raising flour into a large bowl; stir in combined 80g melted butter, 1 cup buttermilk and 1 egg. Add 3 finely chopped green onions and 125g crumbled fetta to flour mixture; fold gently to combine (do not over-mix; mixture should be lumpy). Spoon mixture into pan holes. Bake muffins for 25 minutes or until a skewer inserted into the centre of one comes out clean. Leave in pan for 5 minutes; transfer, top-side up, to a wire rack to cool.

Corn, Zucchini and FETTA

Add a drained 300g can of corn kernels, 1 coarsely grated zucchini squeezed of excess liquid and 120g chopped drained roasted capsicum in oil to green onion and fetta base muffin mixture opposite when adding the fetta. Continue with recipe.

RASPBERRY-CHIA COCONUT SLICE

PREP + COOK TIME *50 MINUTES (+ STANDING & COOLING)* **MAKES** *18*

90g butter, softened

½ cup (110g) caster sugar

1 egg

⅔ cup (100g) plain flour

⅓ cup (50g) self-raising flour

RASPBERRY-CHIA JAM

250g fresh or frozen raspberries

1 tbsp white chia seeds

2 tsp pure maple syrup

COCONUT TOPPING

2 eggs

2 cups (160g) desiccated coconut

⅓ cup (75g) caster sugar

1 Make raspberry-chia jam.

2 Meanwhile, preheat oven to 180°C/160°C fan-forced. Grease a 19cm x 29cm slice pan; line with baking paper, extending paper 5cm over long sides.

3 Beat butter, sugar and egg in a small bowl with an electric mixer until light and fluffy; stir in sifted flours in two batches.

4 Spread pastry mixture over base of pan. Spread raspberry-chia jam evenly over top.

5 Make coconut topping. Spread topping over jam.

6 Bake slice for 35 minutes or until base is cooked and top is golden. Cool in pan. Cut into 18 squares or rectangles.

RASPBERRY-CHIA JAM Process raspberries until a smooth puree forms; transfer to a small bowl and stir in chia and maple syrup. Stand for 20 minutes or until thickened. Makes about ¾ cup.

COCONUT TOPPING Beat eggs lightly with a fork; stir in coconut and sugar until well combined.

SWAP IT Use ½ cup raspberry, strawberry or apricot jam instead of making the raspberry-chia jam, if preferred. Alternatively, you could use blueberries instead of raspberries in the jam. Use 1 cup desiccated coconut and 1 cup almond meal instead of 2 cups desiccated coconut in the topping.

PREP IT Slice can be made up to 5 days in advance and stored in an airtight container.

Energy balls three ways

PREP TIME *20 MINUTES EACH VARIATION (+ REFRIGERATION)*
MAKES *22 JAFFA 'TRUFFLE', 32 APPLE CRUMBLE & 26 'BROWNIE'*

Jaffa 'truffle'

1 cup (90g) rolled oats
12 fresh dates (240g), pitted
½ cup (40g) shredded coconut
1 tsp finely grated orange rind
1 tsp vanilla bean paste
½ cup dutch-processed cocoa
   powder or cacao powder,
   for rolling

Apple crumble

150g medjool dates, pitted
1½ tbsp lemon juice
1 tsp ground cinnamon
1⅔ cups (150g) rolled oats
2 cups dried apple (110g)
½ cup (100g) pepitas
½ cup shredded coconut,
   for rolling

'Brownie'

125g natural almonds, chopped finely
125g medjool dates, pitted
100g dark roasted sugar-free peanut butter
2 tbsp coconut oil, melted
1 tbsp cacao powder
½ tsp ground cinnamon
½ tsp pure vanilla extract
75g finely chopped natural almonds, extra, for rolling

1 For each energy ball, pulse ingredients, except the last in each list, in a food processor until they clump together; do not over-process the mixture.
2 With damp hands, roll 2 level teaspoons of mixture into balls.
3 For jaffa 'truffle' balls, roll in cocoa powder. For apple crumble balls, roll in coconut. For 'brownie' balls, roll in the extra chopped almonds. Place energy balls on an oven tray lined with baking paper; refrigerate for 1 hour to firm.

PREP IT Energy balls can be made up to 2 weeks in advance and refrigerated in an airtight container.

SMOKED SALMON SUSHI CUPS

PREP + COOK TIME 30 MINUTES   **MAKES** 12

2 x 250g packets microwave
   brown and red rice

¼ cup (75g) japanese
   mayonnaise

3 tsp rice wine vinegar

¼ cup (35g) sunflower seeds,
   chopped finely

6 sheets toasted seaweed
   (nori)

100g smoked salmon slices

½ medium avocado, diced finely

1 tsp lemon juice

½ lebanese cucumber,
   diced finely

1 Microwave rice following packet directions; transfer
to a bowl.

2 Process half the rice until chopped coarsely; return
to remaining rice. Add mayonnaise, vinegar and seeds;
stir to combine.

3 Grease and line a 12-hole (⅓-cup/80ml) muffin pan with
cupcake liners. Cut nori sheets lengthways into four strips
each. Cut each strip in half. Place 4 nori strips in each hole,
shiny-side down, forming a cross pattern. Divide rice mixture
among holes; top with salmon.

4 Combine avocado and lemon juice in a small bowl. Top
half the sushi cups with avocado mixture; top the remaining
sushi cups with cucumber. Refrigerate until ready to eat.

SWAP IT   Use your favourite mayonnaise instead of
japanese mayonnaise, if preferred.

PREP IT   Make sushi cups the night before or in
the morning.

TAKE IT   Pack serving-sized portions of sushi cups in
airtight containers. Transport in cooler bags. Refrigerate
until ready to serve.

SERVE IT   Serve sushi cups with edamame pods.

Gluten Free

BANANA and APRICOT LOAF

PREP + COOK TIME 1 HOUR 15 MINUTES (+ COOLING) **SERVES** 8

1 cup (260g) mashed ripe
  banana (see tips)
¾ cup (180ml) buttermilk
2 tsp vanilla extract
2 cups (300g) wholemeal
  self-raising flour
1 tsp bicarbonate of soda
1½ tsp baking powder
1½ tsp ground cinnamon
1⅓ cups (200g) dried apricots,
  chopped coarsely
1 cup (110g) toasted muesli
  (see tips)
80g butter, melted
2 eggs, beaten lightly

1 Preheat oven to 180°C/160°C fan-forced. Grease a 14cm x 24cm (top measurement) loaf pan; line with baking paper, extending paper 5cm over long sides.

2 Place banana, buttermilk and vanilla in a bowl; stir until well combined.

3 Sift flour, soda, baking powder and cinnamon into a large bowl; return husks to bowl. Add apricot and half the muesli to flour mixture; mix well. Add banana mixture, butter and egg to flour mixture; fold gently to combine. Spoon batter into pan; level surface. Scatter with remaining muesli.

4 Bake loaf for 45 minutes or until a skewer inserted into the centre comes out clean. Stand in pan for 15 minutes; using baking paper, lift carefully, top-side up, onto a wire rack to cool completely.

TIPS   You will need about 3 medium over-ripe bananas. We used a fruit-free muesli to prevent the crunchy top from burning.

SWAP IT   Use dates instead of the apricots and melted coconut oil instead of the butter, if preferred.

PREP IT   Loaf can be made up to 5 days in advance and stored in an airtight container.

SERVE IT   Serve slices of loaf spread with a little ricotta, drizzled with pure maple syrup or honey.

CARROT CAKE MUFFINS

PREP + COOK TIME 35 MINUTES (+ COOLING) **MAKES** 12

¾ cup (110g) self-raising flour
½ cup (75g) plain flour
¾ tsp bicarbonate of soda
⅓ cup (75g) caster sugar
¾ tsp ground cinnamon
440g can crushed pineapple,
    drained well
175g firmly packed grated
    carrot (see tip)
100ml vegetable oil
1 large egg, beaten lightly

COCONUT CRUST
1½ cups (115g) shredded
    coconut
¼ cup (55g) brown sugar
1 egg, beaten lightly

1 Preheat oven to 180°C/160°C fan-forced. Grease a 12-hole (⅓-cup/80ml) muffin pan.
2 Sift flours, soda, sugar and cinnamon into a medium bowl; add pineapple and carrot. Stir in combined oil and egg; do not over-mix. Divide mixture among pan holes.
3 Bake muffins for 10 minutes.
4 Meanwhile, make coconut crust.
5 Spoon crust over muffins; return to oven. Bake for a further 15 minutes or until a skewer inserted into the centre of one comes out clean. Stand muffins in pan for 5 minutes; transfer, top-side up, to a wire rack to cool.
COCONUT CRUST Combine ingredients in a bowl.

TIP You will need 2 medium carrots for this recipe.

PREP IT Muffins can be made up to 3 days in advance and stored in an airtight container (refrigerate in humid weather), or wrap muffins individually in plastic wrap and freeze for up to 3 months.

Choc-beetroot slab cake

PREP + COOK TIME 50 MINUTES **MAKES** 18 PIECES

2 large beetroot (400g), peeled
1 cup (250ml) buttermilk
¼ cup (60ml) vegetable oil
1½ tbsp apple cider vinegar
125g butter
1½ cups (330g) caster sugar
2 eggs
2 tsp vanilla bean paste
2½ cups (375g) plain flour
¼ cup (30g) dutch-processed cocoa powder
1½ tsp bicarbonate of soda
1 tsp fine sea salt

1 Preheat oven to 180°C/160°C fan-forced. Grease a 25cm x 37cm slice pan; line with baking paper, extending paper 5cm over long sides.

2 Grate beetroot; you need 2½ cups grated beetroot. Transfer to a food processor and add buttermilk, oil and vinegar; process until as smooth as possible.

3 Meanwhile, beat butter and sugar with an electric mixer until smooth and pale; add one egg at a time, beating well after each addition. With motor operating, add vanilla.

4 Fold in beetroot mixture to combine. Sift flour, cocoa powder, soda and salt into a clean bowl. Add sifted dry ingredients to the beetroot and butter mixture until just incorporated; do not over-mix.

5 Spoon batter into slice pan; bake for 30 minutes or until a skewer comes out clean when inserted in the centre. Stand cake in pan for 5 minutes; transfer to a wire rack to cool completely. Cut cake into 18 pieces.

Prep it Cake can be made up to 5 days in advance and stored in an airtight container, or wrap pieces individually in plastic wrap and freeze for up to 3 months.

CARROT FELAFEL SNACK-PACK

PREP + COOK TIME *35 MINUTES* **SERVES** *6*

2 medium carrots (240g), grated coarsely

400g can chickpeas, drained, rinsed

1 small red onion, chopped finely

1 tsp ground cumin

2 tsp harissa paste

¼ cup (35g) plain flour

½ tsp baking powder

1 egg

1½ cups (225g) panko breadcrumbs

oil, for deep-frying

2 baby cos lettuces, leaves separated

1 lebanese cucumber, sliced thinly into ribbons

2 radishes, sliced thinly

HARISSA YOGHURT

¾ cup (200g) Greek-style yoghurt

½ tsp harissa paste

1 Process carrot, chickpeas, onion, cumin, harissa, flour, baking powder and egg until mixture just comes together; season. Transfer mixture to a large bowl; stir in ¾ cup of the breadcrumbs. Roll level tablespoons of carrot mixture to make about 28 balls. Roll felafel in remaining breadcrumbs to coat.

2 Fill a large saucepan or wok one-third with oil and heat to 180°C (or until a cube of bread turns golden brown in 15 seconds). Deep-fry felafel, in batches, for 2 minutes or until golden and cooked through. Drain on paper towel.

3 Make harissa yoghurt.

4 Serve felafel with harissa yoghurt, lettuce, cucumber and radish. Use lettuce leaves to wrap felafel, if you like.

HARISSA YOGHURT Combine ingredients in a small bowl; season to taste. Makes ¾ cup.

Swap it Omit making the harissa yoghurt and serve with your favourite purchased hummus instead, if you like.

Prep it Felafel can be made up to 3 days in advance and refrigerated in an airtight container. Recipe is not suitable to freeze. Harissa yoghurt can be made the night before or in the morning.

Take it Pack serving-sized portions of felafel and harissa yoghurt in separate airtight containers. Transport in cooler bags. Refrigerate until ready to serve. Reheat felafel in a microwave, if you like.

5
A DAY

EASY GRANOLA BARS

PREP + COOK TIME 55 MINUTES **MAKES** 20

125g unsalted butter,
  chopped coarsely
⅓ cup (75g) firmly packed
  brown sugar
2 tbsp honey
1½ cups (135g) rolled oats
½ cup (75g) self-raising flour
½ cup (75g) dried apricots,
  chopped finely
¼ cup (50g) pepitas
¼ cup (35g) sunflower seeds
8 fresh dates, pitted,
  chopped finely
⅓ cup (25g) shredded coconut

1 Preheat oven to 160°C/140°C fan-forced. Grease an 18cm x 27cm slice pan; line with baking paper, extending paper 5cm over long sides.
2 Stir butter, sugar and honey in a medium saucepan over low heat until sugar dissolves. Stir in remaining ingredients. Press mixture firmly into pan. Bake for 40 minutes or until slice is golden. Cool in pan. Cut into 20 bars.

SWAP IT Use 3 cups (330g) of your favourite muesli instead of the oats, dried fruit, coconut and seeds, if preferred.

PREP IT Granola bars can be made up to 1 week in advance and stored in an airtight container.

WARMING SOUPS

CHICKPEA and COUSCOUS VEGIE SOUP

PREP + COOK TIME 40 MINUTES SERVES 4

1 tbsp extra virgin olive oil

1 red onion, chopped finely

2 cloves garlic, crushed

2 tsp ground cumin

2 tsp ground coriander

1 medium potato, diced

1 large carrot, diced

2 x 400g cans diced tomatoes

400g can chickpeas, drained,
    rinsed

1 litre (4 cups) vegetable stock

1 large zucchini, diced

⅓ cup (65g) couscous

2 tbsp finely chopped
    coriander

coriander leaves, to serve
    (optional)

1 Heat oil in a large heavy-based saucepan over medium heat; cook onion, stirring, for 3 minutes or until softened. Stir in garlic and spices; cook for a further 1 minute or until fragrant.

2 Add potato and carrot; cook, stirring, for 2 minutes or until well coated in spice mixture. Add tomatoes, chickpeas and stock; bring to the boil. Reduce heat to low; cook, covered, for 10 minutes or until vegetables are just tender, adding zucchini during last 5 minutes of cooking. Remove from heat.

3 Stir in couscous and chopped coriander; stand, covered, for 10 minutes or until couscous is tender. Season to taste.

4 Serve soup topped with coriander leaves.

TIP   Soup will thicken on standing, so add a little more stock or boiling water before reheating to achieve the desired consistency.

PREP IT   Soup can be made to the end of step 3 up to 2 days in advance and refrigerated in an airtight container. Or freeze it for up to 3 months; thaw in the fridge, then reheat in a microwave.

TAKE IT   Divide soup among portion-sized airtight containers. Transport in cooler bags. Refrigerate until ready to serve. Reheat in a microwave. Alternatively, reheat soup at home and transport in a thermos.

SERVE IT   Serve soup with buttered toasted turkish bread.

5 A DAY

THAI GREEN CHICKEN CURRY SOUP

PREP + COOK TIME 50 MINUTES **SERVES** 4

1 small head broccoli

1 tbsp olive oil

2 chicken breast fillets, cut into 2.5cm pieces

2 tbsp green curry paste (see tip)

1 litre (4 cups) salt-reduced chicken stock

1 large potato, chopped coarsely

1 medium zucchini, halved lengthways, sliced on the diagonal

150g green beans, trimmed, cut into thirds

115g fresh baby corn, halved lengthways

2 kaffir lime leaves

165ml can coconut milk

1 tbsp lime juice

1 tbsp fish sauce

1 tbsp brown sugar

1 Separate broccoli florets from stem. Peel and dice stem; cut florets into small pieces. Reserve stem and florets in separate bowls.

2 Heat oil in a large heavy-based saucepan over medium heat. Cook chicken, in batches, for 8 minutes or until golden all over. Transfer to a bowl. Add curry paste to pan; cook, stirring, for 2 minutes or until fragrant. Stir in stock until combined.

3 Add broccoli stem and potato; simmer, covered, for 15 minutes or until vegetables are tender. Cool slightly; blend with a stick blender until smooth.

4 Return chicken to pan; simmer for 5 minutes. Add broccoli florets, zucchini, beans, corn and kaffir lime leaves; simmer for 5 minutes. Reduce heat to low; add coconut milk, lime juice, fish sauce and brown sugar. Stir until sugar dissolves; season to taste.

TIP Adjust the amount of curry paste to suit your taste.

SWAP IT You can use chicken thigh fillets instead of breast fillets, if preferred.

PREP IT Soup can be made up to 2 days in advance and refrigerated in an airtight container. Or freeze it for up to 1 month; thaw in the fridge, then reheat in a microwave.

TAKE IT Divide soup among portion-sized airtight containers. Transport in cooler bags. Refrigerate until ready to serve. Reheat in a microwave. Alternatively, reheat soup at home and transport in a thermos.

SERVE IT Top soup with coriander leaves or micro coriander and serve with microwave brown or jasmine rice.

Meat Free

Spiced Pumpkin and Sweet Potato Soup

PREP + COOK TIME 1 HOUR 10 MINUTES **SERVES** 4

2 tbsp extra virgin olive oil

2 onions, chopped coarsely

600g peeled kent pumpkin, chopped coarsely

3 small orange sweet potatoes, chopped coarsely

1 tbsp ground coriander

2 tsp cumin seeds

¼ tsp dried chilli flakes

1 litre (4 cups) vegetable stock

Greek-style yoghurt and coriander sprigs, to serve (optional)

TRAIL MIX CRUNCH

½ cup (60g) pecans

¼ cup (50g) pepitas

1 tbsp sunflower seeds

¼ cup (20g) moist coconut flakes

2 tsp pure maple syrup

½ tsp sea salt flakes

pinch cayenne pepper (optional)

1 Make trail mix crunch.

2 Heat oil in a large saucepan over medium-high heat; cook onion, pumpkin and sweet potato, stirring, for 5 minutes or until onion softens. Add ground coriander, cumin and chilli; cook, stirring, for 1 minute or until fragrant.

3 Add stock and 2 cups (500ml) water to pan; bring to the boil. Reduce heat; simmer, covered, for 30 minutes or until vegetables are tender. Cool soup for 10 minutes.

4 Blend soup, in batches, until smooth. Return to pan; stir over medium-high heat until heated through.

5 Serve soup topped with trail mix crunch, yoghurt and coriander. Season with pepper.

TRAIL MIX CRUNCH Preheat oven to 180°C/160°C fan-forced. Line an oven tray with baking paper. Place ingredients in a bowl; toss to coat well. Spread mixture evenly, in a single layer, across tray. Bake for 10 minutes, stirring halfway through cooking time, or until nut mixture is golden. Cool. Makes 1¼ cups.

Prep it Soup can be made to the end of step 4 up to 3 days in advance and refrigerated in an airtight container. Or freeze it for up to 3 months; thaw in the fridge, then reheat in a microwave. Trail mix crunch can be made up to 2 weeks in advance and stored in an airtight container.

Take it Divide soup among portion-sized airtight containers. Pack trail mix crunch, yoghurt and coriander separately. Transport in cooler bags. Refrigerate until ready to serve. Reheat soup in a microwave; top with trail mix crunch, yoghurt and coriander just before serving. Alternatively, reheat soup at home and transport in a thermos.

SWAP IT To make this nut-free, omit the pecans, pepitas and sunflower seeds and use ¾ cup purchased seed mix (pepitas and sunflower seeds) instead.

Cheat's Pea and Ham Soup

2 tbsp olive oil

1 leek, white part only,
  sliced thinly

1 clove garlic, chopped finely

1 large potato (200g), chopped

1.5 litres (6 cups) chicken stock

6 cups (720g) frozen peas

⅔ cup mint leaves

300g leg ham, sliced thinly

snow pea tendrils, to serve
  (optional)

1 Heat half the oil in a large heavy-based saucepan over low-medium heat; cook leek and garlic, stirring, for 3 minutes or until softened.

2 Add potato, stock and 1 cup (250ml) water; bring to the boil. Reduce heat to low-medium; cook, covered, for 10 minutes or until potato is tender. Add 5 cups (600g) of the peas; cook for a further 2 minutes or until peas are just tender. Remove pan from heat.

3 Add mint to soup; blend with a stick blender until smooth. Add remaining peas; stir over low-medium heat until hot. Season to taste. Reduce heat to low; cover to keep warm.

4 Meanwhile, heat remaining oil in a frying pan over medium heat; cook ham, stirring, for 2 minutes or until golden brown and crisp. Top soup with ham; season to taste. Serve soup topped with snow pea tendrils.

Tips If using a blender or food processor to blend soup rather than a stick blender, stand for 10 minutes to cool slightly before blending, otherwise the heat build-up can cause the lid to come off while blending.

Prep it Soup can be made to the end of step 3 up to 3 days in advance and refrigerated in an airtight container. Or freeze it for up to 3 months; thaw in the fridge, then reheat in a microwave. Continue with step 4.

Take it Divide soup among portion-sized airtight containers. Transport in cooler bags. Refrigerate until ready to serve. Reheat in a microwave. Alternatively, reheat soup at home and transport in a thermos.

CAULIFLOWER and ALMOND SOUP

PREP + COOK TIME 40 MINUTES **SERVES** 6

2 tbsp extra virgin olive oil

4 green onions, trimmed, chopped

2 cloves garlic, crushed

1kg cauliflower, cut into florets

1.5 litres (6 cups) vegetable or chicken stock

1 large desiree potato, chopped coarsely

1 medium fennel bulb, trimmed, chopped coarsely

100g blanched almonds, toasted, chopped coarsely (see tip)

2 tbsp dukkah (optional)

1 Heat oil in a large heavy-based saucepan over medium heat; cook green onion, stirring, for 2 minutes or until softened. Add garlic and cauliflower; cook for 30 seconds.

2 Increase heat to high. Add stock, potato and fennel; bring to the boil. Reduce heat to low; cook, covered, for 20 minutes or until vegetables are tender. Cool for 5 minutes.

3 Blend soup and almonds, in batches if necessary, until smooth and creamy; season to taste.

4 Serve soup sprinkled with dukkah.

Tip To achieve a smooth and creamy consistency, it is important to coarsely chop the almonds before adding them to the blender.

Prep it Soup can be made to the end of step 3 up to 2 days in advance and refrigerated in an airtight container. Or freeze it for up to 3 months; thaw in the fridge, then reheat in a microwave.

Take it Divide soup among portion-sized airtight containers. Transport in cooler bags. Refrigerate until ready to serve. Reheat in a microwave. Alternatively, reheat soup at home and transport in a thermos. Pack dukkah separately and sprinkle on soup just before serving.

Serve it Serve soup with purchased cheese pastry twists for dipping.

MEAT
FREE

5
A DAY

SPICED MOROCCAN CHICKEN NOODLE SOUP

PREP + COOK TIME 1 HOUR 30 MINUTES **SERVES** 8

2 tbsp extra virgin olive oil

1 large onion, chopped finely

4 cloves garlic, crushed

3 tsp ground cumin

3 tsp ground coriander

3 tsp sweet paprika

1 tsp turmeric

¼ tsp cayenne pepper
   (optional)

2 litres (8 cups) chicken stock

2 chicken breast fillets

4 medium carrots,
   chopped finely

2 trimmed celery stalks,
   chopped finely

1 medium orange sweet potato,
   diced finely

4 large tomatoes, diced

400g can chickpeas,
   drained, rinsed

90g dried egg noodles

Greek-style yoghurt and mint
   leaves, to serve (optional)

1 Heat oil in a large heavy-based saucepan over medium heat. Cook onion for 6 minutes or until golden. Add garlic; cook for a further 2 minutes. Add spices; cook, stirring, for 2 minutes or until fragrant.

2 Add stock, chicken, carrot, celery, sweet potato and tomato; bring to the boil. Reduce heat to low; cook for 15 minutes or until chicken is cooked through. Remove chicken; cool. When cool enough to handle, shred chicken; reserve. Continue to simmer soup for a further 45 minutes or until vegetables are tender.

3 Partially puree soup with a stick blender until thickened but some texture still remains. Stir through shredded chicken, chickpeas and noodles; cook, covered, for 8 minutes or until noodles are cooked through.

4 Top soup with yoghurt and mint to serve; season to taste.

SWAP IT Use two 400g cans diced tomatoes instead of fresh tomatoes, if preferred.

PREP IT Soup can be made to the end of step 3 up to 2 days in advance and refrigerated in an airtight container. Or freeze it for up to 3 months; thaw in the fridge, then reheat in a microwave.

TAKE IT Divide soup among portion-sized airtight containers. Transport in cooler bags. Refrigerate until ready to serve. Reheat in a microwave. Alternatively, reheat soup at home and transport in a thermos.

CHILLI CON CARNE SOUP

PREP + COOK TIME *35 MINUTES* SERVES *6*

1 bunch coriander

2 tbsp olive oil

1 red onion, chopped finely

2 cloves garlic, crushed

35g sachet fajita seasoning mix

500g lean minced beef

400g bottled tomato and chilli
   pasta sauce

1.5 litres (6 cups) beef stock

400g can red kidney beans,
   drained, rinsed

tortilla chips and sour cream,
   to serve (optional)

1 Separate coriander roots, stems and leaves. Wash and finely chop roots, stems and half the leaves; reserve remaining leaves to serve.

2 Heat oil in a large heavy-based saucepan over medium heat; cook onion, stirring, for 3 minutes or until softened. Stir in chopped coriander, garlic and seasoning mix; cook for 1 minute or until fragrant.

3 Increase heat to high and add mince; cook, stirring to break up any clumps, for 5 minutes or until well browned. Add pasta sauce, stock and beans; bring to the boil. Reduce heat to low; cook, covered, for 10 minutes. Skim and discard fat from surface. Season to taste.

4 Serve soup with tortilla chips, sour cream and topped with reserved coriander leaves.

PREP IT Soup can be made to the end of step 3 up to 2 days in advance and refrigerated in an airtight container. Or freeze it for up to 3 months; thaw in the fridge, then reheat in a microwave.

TAKE IT Divide soup among portion-sized airtight containers. Transport in cooler bags. Refrigerate until ready to serve. Reheat in a microwave. Alternatively, reheat soup at home and transport in a thermos.

CHEAP EAT

Carrot and Hazelnut Soup with Lunch Box Crunch

PREP + COOK TIME 45 MINUTES **SERVES 4**

2 tbsp extra virgin olive oil

1 large onion, chopped coarsely

2 cloves garlic, chopped coarsely

800g carrots, chopped coarsely

½ cup (70g) skinless roasted hazelnuts

2 tbsp thyme leaves

1.5 litres (6 cups) vegetable stock

1 tbsp red wine vinegar

LUNCH BOX CRUNCH

⅓ cup (45g) skinless roasted hazelnuts, chopped coarsely

¼ cup (50g) pepitas

70g crushed tortilla chips

½ tsp smoked paprika

olive oil spray

1 Heat oil in a large heavy-based saucepan over low heat. Cook onion and garlic, stirring, for 5 minutes or until softened.

2 Stir in carrot, hazelnuts and thyme; cook for 1 minute or until thyme is fragrant. Add stock and increase heat to medium; bring to a simmer. Cook, covered, for 15 minutes or until carrot is tender. Stand for 10 minutes.

3 Meanwhile, make lunch box crunch.

4 Add vinegar to soup; blend or process, in batches if necessary, until a smooth puree forms. Season to taste.

5 Top soup with lunch box crunch just before serving.

LUNCH BOX CRUNCH Preheat oven to 180°C/160°C fan-forced. Line an oven tray with baking paper. Combine ingredients, except oil spray, in a small bowl; spread on lined tray and spray with oil. Bake for 8 minutes; cool.

SWAP IT To make this nut-free, omit the hazelnuts from the soup and add 1 tablespoon tahini in step 4, and use ⅓ cup sunflower seeds instead of hazelnuts in the lunch box crunch.

PREP IT Soup can be made to the end of step 4 up to 2 days in advance. Or freeze it for up to 3 months; thaw in the fridge, then reheat in a microwave. Lunch box crunch can be made up to 1 week in advance and stored in an airtight container.

TAKE IT Divide soup among portion-sized airtight containers. Pack lunch box crunch separately. Transport in cooler bags. Refrigerate until ready to take. Reheat soup in a microwave; top with lunch box crunch just before serving. Alternatively, reheat soup at home and transport in a thermos.

Hearty Chicken Soup with Last-Minute Add-Ins

PREP + COOK TIME 1 HOUR 15 MINUTES **SERVES** 6

3 trimmed celery stalks, quartered

1 large carrot, quartered

1 small red capsicum, quartered, seeded

2 cloves garlic

1 tbsp lemon thyme leaves

1 tsp dried oregano

2 tbsp extra virgin olive oil

1kg chicken thigh fillets, trimmed of excess fat

1 litre (4 cups) chicken stock

¼ cup (50g) pearl couscous

OPTIONAL ADD-INS FOR ONE

125g can corn kernels, drained

100g green beans, chopped

½ small zucchini, diced finely

1 Pulse celery, carrot, capsicum, garlic and herbs in a food processor until chopped coarsely.

2 Heat oil in a large heavy-based saucepan over high heat. Cook vegetable mixture, stirring occasionally, for 3 minutes or until softened slightly.

3 Add chicken carefully to pan. Add stock and stir gently; bring to a simmer, then reduce heat to medium. Cook, covered, for 45 minutes or until chicken is tender and almost falling apart. Transfer chicken to a plate. Skim and discard fat from surface of soup. Using two forks, shred chicken; return to soup.

4 Remove soup from heat; stir in couscous. Stand, covered, for 10 minutes or until couscous is tender. Season to taste.

5 Add your chosen add-in to the soup; heat. Season to taste.

Prep it Soup can be made to the end of step 4 up to 3 days in advance and refrigerated in an airtight container. Or freeze it for up to 3 months; thaw in the fridge, then reheat in a microwave.

Take it Divide soup among portion-sized airtight containers and pack your chosen add-in/s separately. Transport in cooler bags. Refrigerate until ready to serve. Add add-ins to soup just before reheating in a microwave. Alternatively, reheat soup at home and transport in a thermos.

5 A DAY

TIP Soup will thicken on standing, so add a little more stock or boiling water before reheating to achieve the desired consistency.

SERVE IT Serve soup with some crusty bread.

CHEAP
EAT

CREAMY BROCCOLI SOUP WITH QUINOA CRUNCH

PREP + COOK TIME 35 MINUTES SERVES 4

1 tbsp extra virgin olive oil

1 leek, white part only,
   sliced thinly

2 trimmed sticks celery,
   chopped finely

2 cloves garlic, crushed

1 large head broccoli,
   cut into florets

2 zucchini, chopped coarsely

1 large potato, chopped coarsely

3 cups (750ml) vegetable stock

QUINOA CRUNCH

½ cup (100g) white quinoa,
   rinsed well

2 tbsp extra virgin olive oil

2 tbsp sunflower seeds

2 tbsp coarsely chopped
   roasted almonds or pepitas

1 tsp chilli flakes (optional)

2 cloves garlic, crushed

2 tbsp finely chopped
   flat-leaf parsley

1 Heat oil in a large heavy-based saucepan over medium-high heat. Cook leek and celery, stirring, for 3 minutes or until softened. Add garlic; cook for 1 minute or until fragrant.

2 Add broccoli, zucchini, potato, stock and 2 cups (500ml) water; bring to the boil. Reduce heat to low-medium; simmer for 10 minutes or until vegetables are tender. Remove soup from heat; cool slightly.

3 Meanwhile, make quinoa crunch.

4 Blend or process soup until smooth. Season to taste.

5 Serve soup topped with quinoa crunch.

QUINOA CRUNCH Cook rinsed quinoa following packet directions; drain. Heat oil in a medium frying pan over medium heat; add quinoa, sunflower seeds, almonds and chilli flakes. Cook, stirring, for 10 minutes or until quinoa becomes golden. Add garlic and parsley; cook, stirring, for 1 minute or until fragrant. Transfer to a plate to cool; it will crisp as it cools.

PREP IT Soup can be made to the end of step 4 up to 2 days in advance and refrigerated in an airtight container. Or freeze it for up to 3 months; thaw in the fridge, then reheat in a microwave.

TAKE IT Divide soup among portion-sized airtight containers and pack quinoa crunch separately. Transport in cooler bags. Refrigerate until ready to serve. Reheat soup in a microwave; top with quinoa crunch just before serving. Alternatively, reheat soup at home and transport in a thermos.

SERVE IT Serve soup with chargrilled or toasted sourdough bread drizzled with extra virgin olive oil.

CURRIED LENTIL VEGIE SOUP

PREP + COOK TIME 55 MINUTES **SERVES** 4

½ **bunch coriander**

1 **tbsp extra virgin olive oil**

1 **onion, chopped finely**

2 **cloves garlic, crushed**

1 **fresh long red chilli, seeded,**
   chopped finely

4cm **piece fresh ginger,**
   grated finely

1 **tsp ground turmeric**

1 **tsp ground cumin**

1 **tsp garam masala**

2 **fresh bay leaves**

1 **cup (150g) red lentils**

300g **kent pumpkin,**
   chopped coarsely

4 **medium tomatoes, seeded,**
   diced finely

1 **litre (4 cups) salt-reduced**
   vegetable stock

60g **baby spinach leaves,**
   trimmed

1 Separate coriander roots, stems and leaves. Wash and finely chop roots and stems (reserve leaves for another use).

2 Heat oil in a large heavy-based saucepan over medium heat. Add chopped coriander, onion, garlic, chilli and ginger; cook, stirring, for 4 minutes or until softened. Add turmeric, cumin, garam masala and bay leaves; cook, stirring, for 1 minute or until fragrant.

3 Add lentils, pumpkin, tomato, stock and 2 cups (500ml) water to pan; bring to the boil over high heat. Reduce heat to low; cook, covered, for 25 minutes or until lentils and pumpkin are very tender. Remove lid; cook for a further 10 minutes or until thickened, adding spinach for the last 2 minutes of cooking time.

PREP IT Soup can be made up to 2 days in advance and refrigerated in an airtight container. Or freeze it for up to 3 months; thaw in the fridge, then reheat in a microwave.

TAKE IT Divide soup among portion-sized airtight containers. Transport in cooler bags. Refrigerate until ready to serve. Reheat in a microwave. Alternatively, reheat soup at home and transport in a thermos.

SERVE IT Serve soup with chargrilled plain or garlic naan bread and Greek-style yoghurt.

MEAT FREE

Meatball and Risoni Soup

PREP + COOK TIME 45 MINUTES SERVES 4

500g pork and fennel sausages

½ cup (50g) fresh breadcrumbs

2 cloves garlic, crushed

⅓ cup (25g) finely grated
  parmesan

¼ cup finely chopped
  flat-leaf parsley

2 tbsp extra virgin olive oil

1 small onion, chopped finely

1 bunch cavolo nero, leaves
  picked, torn coarsely

2 litres (8 cups) chicken stock

1 cup (220g) risoni

1 tbsp chopped dill

1 Preheat oven to 200°C/180°C fan-forced. Grease and line a large oven tray.

2 Remove sausage meat from casings; discard casings. Place sausage meat, breadcrumbs, garlic, parmesan and half the parsley in a large bowl; season. Using clean hands, mix until sausage meat is broken down and ingredients are well combined. Roll heaped tablespoons of mixture to make 16 balls in total; spread across prepared tray. Bake meatballs for 25 minutes or until cooked through and golden brown.

3 Meanwhile, heat oil in a large heavy-based saucepan over medium heat. Cook onion, stirring, for 3 minutes or until softened. Add cavolo nero; cook, stirring, for 1 minute. Add chicken stock; bring to the boil.

4 Add risoni to pan; cook for 5 minutes or until just tender. Add meatballs, remaining parsley and dill. Season to taste.

PREP IT Soup can be made up to 3 days in advance and refrigerated in an airtight container. Or freeze it for up to 1 month; thaw in the fridge, then reheat in a microwave. The pasta may absorb some of the stock on standing; add a little boiling water to thin, if you like.

TAKE IT Divide soup among portion-sized airtight containers. Transport in cooler bags. Refrigerate until ready to serve. Reheat in a microwave. Alternatively, reheat soup at home and transport in a thermos.

Roasted Tomato Soup with Broccoli Pesto

PREP + COOK TIME 1 HOUR SERVES 4

1kg vine-ripened tomatoes, quartered

1 onion, chopped coarsely

3 cloves garlic, unpeeled

3 sprigs thyme

½ tsp sea salt flakes

¼ cup (60ml) extra virgin olive oil

3 cups (750ml) vegetable or chicken stock

1 tbsp pine nuts, toasted (optional)

baby basil leaves, to serve (optional)

BROCCOLI PESTO

100g broccoli, chopped coarsely

1 clove garlic, crushed

1½ tbsp pine nuts, toasted

1½ tbsp finely grated parmesan

1½ tbsp coarsely chopped basil

¼ cup (60ml) extra virgin olive oil

1 Preheat oven to 220°C/200°C fan-forced.

2 Place tomato, onion, garlic and thyme in a roasting pan; sprinkle with salt and season with pepper. Drizzle with oil; toss to coat tomato. Roast for 30 minutes or until tomato is very soft and coloured around the edges.

3 Meanwhile, make broccoli pesto.

4 Transfer roasted tomato mixture to a medium saucepan. Squeeze garlic out of skins; add to tomato mixture. Remove and discard thyme stalks. Add stock to pan and bring to the boil; remove from heat and stand for 10 minutes to cool slightly. Blend or process mixture until smooth. Return soup to pan; stir over low heat until hot. Season.

5 Scatter pine nuts and basil over soup. Serve topped with spoonfuls of basil pesto.

BROCCOLI PESTO Add broccoli to a small saucepan of boiling water. Return to the boil; simmer for 2 minutes. Drain, then refresh in cold water; drain well. Process broccoli, garlic, pine nuts, parmesan and basil until finely chopped. With motor operating, gradually pour in oil; process until combined. Season to taste.

Prep it Soup and pesto can be made to the end of step 4 up to 3 days in advance and refrigerated, separately, in airtight containers. Or freeze both for up to 3 months; thaw in the fridge, then reheat soup in a microwave.

Take it Divide soup among portion-sized airtight containers and pack pesto separately. Transport in cooler bags. Refrigerate until ready to serve. Reheat soup in a microwave; top with pesto just before serving. Alternatively, reheat soup at home and transport in a thermos.

Cheap Eat

SWAP IT To make this nut-free, omit the pine nuts and use sunflower seeds in the pesto and for serving. Or skip making the pesto and serve soup with your favourite purchased pesto.

GLOSSARY

ALMONDS flat, pointy-tipped nuts with a pitted brown shell enclosing a creamy white kernel which is covered by a brown skin.
blanched brown skins removed.
meal also called ground almonds.

ANCHOVIES small oily fish. Anchovy fillets are preserved and packed in oil or salt in small cans or jars, and are strong in flavour. Fresh anchovies are much milder in flavour.

BARLEY a nutritious grain used in soups and stews. Hulled barley, the least processed, is high in fibre. Pearl barley has had the husk removed then been steamed and polished so that only the 'pearl' of the original grain remains, much the same as white rice.

BAY LEAVES aromatic leaves from the bay tree available fresh or dried; adds a strong, slightly peppery flavour.

BEANS
broad also known as fava, windsor and horse beans; fresh and frozen beans should be peeled twice (discarding both the outer long green pod and the beige-green tough inner shell).
cannellini small white bean similar in appearance and flavour to other phaseolus vulgaris varieties (great northern, navy or haricot). Available dried or canned.
kidney medium-size red bean, slightly floury in texture yet sweet in flavour. Sold dried or canned; found in bean mixes and is used in chilli con carne.

BICARBONATE OF SODA a raising agent.

BREADCRUMBS
fresh bread processed into crumbs.
panko also known as japanese breadcrumbs. They are available in two types: larger pieces and fine crumbs. Both have a lighter texture than Western-style breadcrumbs. They are available from Asian grocery stores and larger supermarkets.

BROCCOLINI a cross between broccoli and chinese kale; it has long asparagus-like stems with a long loose floret, both are edible. Resembles broccoli but is milder and sweeter in taste.

BUTTER use salted or unsalted (sweet) butter; 125g (4oz) is equal to one stick of butter.

BUTTERMILK originally the term given to the slightly sour liquid left after butter was churned from cream, today it is made from no-fat or low-fat milk to which specific bacterial cultures have been added. Despite its name, it is actually low in fat.

CAPERS grey-green buds of a warm climate shrub (usually Mediterranean), sold either dried and salted or pickled in a vinegar brine.

CARDAMOM a spice native to India and used extensively in its cuisine; can be purchased in pod, seed or ground form. Has a distinctive aromatic, sweetly rich flavour.

CASHEWS plump, kidney-shaped, golden-brown nuts with a distinctive sweet, buttery flavour and containing about 48% fat.

CHEESE
bocconcini from the diminutive of 'boccone', meaning 'mouthful' in Italian; walnut-sized, baby mozzarella, a delicate, semi-soft, white cheese traditionally made from buffalo milk. Sold fresh, it spoils rapidly so will only keep, refrigerated in brine, for 1 or 2 days at the most.
brie soft-ripened cow's milk cheese with a delicate, creamy texture and a rich, sweet taste that varies from buttery to mushroomy. Best served at room temperature after a brief period of ageing, brie should have a bloomy white rind and creamy, voluptuous centre which becomes runny with ripening.
cheddar the most common cow's milk 'tasty' cheese; should be aged, hard and have a pronounced bite.

cream commonly called philadelphia or philly; a soft cow's milk cheese, its fat content ranges from 14 to 33%.

fetta Greek in origin; a crumbly textured goat's or sheep's milk cheese with a sharp, salty taste. Ripened and stored in salted whey; particularly good cubed and tossed into salads.

goat's made from goat's milk, has an earthy, strong taste; available in both soft and firm textures, in various shapes and sizes, and sometimes rolled in ash or herbs.

haloumi a firm, cream-coloured sheep's milk cheese matured in brine; haloumi can be grilled or fried, briefly, without breaking down. Should be eaten while still warm as it becomes rubbery on cooling.

mascarpone an Italian fresh cultured-cream product made in much the same way as yoghurt. Whiteish to creamy yellow in colour, with a buttery-rich, luscious texture.

mozzarella soft, spun-curd cheese; originating in southern Italy where it was traditionally made from water-buffalo milk. Now generally made from cow's milk, it is the most popular pizza cheese because of its low melting point and elasticity when heated.

parmesan also called parmigiano; is a hard, grainy cow's milk cheese originating in the Parma region of Italy. The curd for this cheese is salted in brine for a month, then aged for up to 2 years.

ricotta a soft, sweet, moist, white cow's milk cheese with a low fat content and a slightly grainy texture. The name roughly translates as 'cooked again' and refers to ricotta's manufacture from a whey that is itself a by-product of other cheese making.

CHIA SEEDS contain protein and all the essential amino acids, as well as being fibre rich and a wealth of vitamins, minerals and antioxidants.

CHICKPEAS an irregularly round, sandy-coloured legume. Has a firm texture even after cooking, a floury mouth-feel and robust nutty flavour; available canned or dried (soak for several hours in cold water before use).

CHILLI generally, the smaller the chilli, the hotter it is, Use rubber gloves when seeding and chopping fresh chillies as they can burn your skin. Removing seeds and membranes lessens the heat level.

cayenne pepper a long, thin-fleshed, extremely hot red chilli usually sold dried and ground.

chipotle (pronounced cheh-pote-lay) The name used for jalapeño chillies once they've been dried and smoked. They have a deep, intensely smokey flavour, rather than a searing heat, and are dark brown, almost black in colour and wrinkled in appearance.

flakes also sold as crushed chilli; dehydrated deep-red extremely fine slices and whole seeds from the chilli.

jalapeño (pronounced hah-lah-pain-yo) Fairly hot, medium-sized, plump, dark green chilli; available pickled – sold canned or bottled – and fresh, from greengrocers.

long red available both fresh and dried; a generic term used for any moderately hot, long, thin chilli (about 6cm to 8cm long).

powder the Asian variety is the hottest, made from dried ground thai chillies; can be used instead of fresh in the proportion of ½ teaspoon chilli powder to 1 medium chopped fresh red chilli.

CHORIZO sausage of Spanish origin, made of coarsely ground pork and highly seasoned with garlic and chilli. They are deeply smoked, very spicy. You can buy fresh and dry-cured and both need to be cooked.

CINNAMON available both in the piece (called sticks or quills) and ground into powder; one of the world's most common spices, used universally as a sweet, fragrant flavouring for both sweet and savoury foods. The dried inner bark of the shoots of the Sri Lankan native cinnamon tree; much of what is sold as the real thing is in fact cassia, Chinese cinnamon, from the bark of the cassia tree. Less expensive to process than true cinnamon, it is often blended with Sri Lankan cinnamon to produce the type of 'cinnamon' most commonly found in supermarkets.

COCOA POWDER also called unsweetened cocoa; cocoa beans (cacao seeds) that have been fermented, roasted, shelled, ground into powder then cleared of most of the fat content.

COCONUT

desiccated concentrated, dried, unsweetened and finely shredded coconut flesh.

flaked dried flaked coconut flesh.

milk not the liquid inside the fruit (coconut water), but the diluted liquid from the second pressing of the white flesh of a mature coconut. Available in cans and cartons at most supermarkets.

shredded unsweetened thin strips of dried coconut flesh.

CORIANDER also known as pak chee or chinese parsley; a bright-green leafy herb with a pungent flavour. Both stems and roots of coriander are also used in cooking; wash well before using. Also available ground or as seeds; these should not be substituted for fresh as the tastes are completely different.

COUSCOUS a fine, dehydrated, grain-like cereal product made from semolina; it swells to three or four times its original size when liquid is added. It is eaten like rice with a tagine, as a side dish or salad ingredient.

CRANBERRIES available dried and frozen; have a rich, astringent flavour and can be used in sweet and savoury dishes. The dried version can usually be substituted for or with other dried fruit.

CUMIN also known as zeera or comino; resembling caraway in size, cumin is the dried seed of a plant related to the parsley family.

CURRY POWDER a blend of ground spices used for making Indian and some South-East Asian dishes. It consists of dried chilli, cumin, cinnamon, coriander, fennel, mace, fenugreek, cardamom and turmeric. Available mild or hot.

DUKKAH an Egyptian specialty spice mixture made up of roasted nuts, seeds and an array of aromatic spices.

EDAMAME (SOY BEANS) are fresh soy beans in the pod; available frozen from Asian food stores and major supermarkets.

EGGS we use large chicken eggs weighing an average of 60g unless stated otherwise in the recipes in this book. If a recipe calls for raw or barely cooked eggs, exercise caution if there is a salmonella problem in your area, particularly in food eaten by children and pregnant women.

FENNEL also known as finocchio or anise; a white to very pale green-white, firm, crisp, roundish vegetable. The bulb has a slightly sweet, anise flavour but the leaves have a much stronger taste. Also the name of dried seeds that have a licorice flavour.

FILLO PASTRY paper-thin sheets of raw pastry; brush each sheet with oil or melted butter, stack in layers, then cut and fold as directed.

FISH SAUCE called naam pla on the label if Thai-made, nuoc naam if Vietnamese; the two are almost identical. Made from pulverised salted fermented fish (most often anchovies); has a pungent smell and strong taste.

FLOUR

plain a general all-purpose wheat flour.

rice very fine, almost powdery, gluten-free flour; made from ground white rice. Used in baking, as a thickener, and in some Asian noodles and desserts.

self-raising plain flour sifted with baking powder in the proportion of 1 cup flour to 2 teaspoons baking powder.

wholemeal also known as wholewheat flour; milled with the wheat germ so is higher in fibre and more nutritional than plain flour.

GARAM MASALA a blend of spices that includes cardamom, cloves, cinnamon, coriander, fennel and cumin. Black pepper and chilli can also be added for heat.

GINGER, FRESH also called green or root ginger; the thick gnarled root of a tropical plant. Can be kept, peeled, covered with dry sherry in a jar and refrigerated, or frozen in an airtight container.

HARISSA a Moroccan paste made from dried chillies, cumin, garlic, oil and caraway seeds. Available from Middle Eastern food shops and supermarkets.

HAZELNUTS also known as filberts; plump, grape-sized, rich, sweet nut with a brown skin.

HONEY the variety sold in a squeezable container is not suitable for the recipes in this book.

KAFFIR LIME LEAVES also known as bai magrood and looks like two glossy dark green leaves joined end to end, forming a rounded hourglass shape. Used fresh or dried in many South-East Asian dishes, they are used like bay leaves or curry leaves, especially in Thai cooking. Sold fresh, dried or frozen, the dried leaves are less potent so double the number if using them as a substitute for fresh; a strip of fresh lime peel may be substituted for each kaffir lime leaf.

LEMON GRASS a tall, clumping, lemon-smelling and -tasting, sharp-edged grass; the white part of the stem is used, finely chopped, in cooking.

LENTILS (red, brown, yellow) dried pulses often identified by and named after their colour. Eaten by cultures all over the world, most famously perhaps in the dhals of India, lentils have high food value.

French-style related to the famous French lentils du puy; these green-blue, tiny lentils have a nutty, earthy flavour and a hardy nature that allows them to be rapidly cooked without disintegrating.

MAPLE SYRUP, PURE distilled from the sap of sugar maple trees found only in Canada and the USA. Maple-flavoured syrup or pancake syrup is not an adequate substitute for the real thing.

MIRIN a Japanese champagne-coloured cooking wine, made of glutinous rice and alcohol. It is used expressly for cooking and should not be confused with sake.

MISO fermented soy bean paste. There are many types of miso, each with its own aroma, flavour, colour and texture; it can be kept, airtight, for up to a year in the fridge.

MUSTARD
dijon pale brown, distinctively flavoured, fairly mild-tasting French mustard.

wholegrain also known as seeded. A French-style coarse-grain mustard made from crushed mustard seeds and Dijon-style French mustard.

NORI a type of dried seaweed used in Japanese cooking as a flavouring, garnish or for sushi. Sold in thin sheets, plain or toasted (yaki-nori).

OIL
olive made from ripened olives. Extra virgin and virgin are the first and second press, respectively, of the olives; 'light' refers to taste not fat levels.

sesame made from roasted, crushed, white sesame seeds; used as a flavouring rather than a cooking oil.

ONION
green also called, incorrectly, shallot; an immature onion picked before the bulb has formed. Has a long, bright-green edible stalk.
red also known as spanish, red spanish or bermuda onion; a sweet-flavoured, large, purple-red onion.
shallots also called french or golden shallots or eschalots; small and brown-skinned.

PANCETTA an Italian unsmoked bacon. Pork belly cured in salt and spices then rolled into a sausage shape and dried for several weeks.

PAPRIKA ground, dried, sweet red capsicum (bell pepper); there are many grades and types available, including sweet, hot, mild and smoked.

PEPITAS are the pale green kernels of dried pumpkin seeds; they can be bought plain or salted.

PINE NUTS not a nut but a small, cream coloured kernel from pine cones. Toast before use to bring out their flavour.

PISTACHIOS green, delicately flavoured nuts inside hard off-white shells. Available salted or unsalted in their shells; you can also get them shelled.

POMEGRANATE dark-red, leathery-skinned fruit about the size of an orange filled with hundreds of seeds, each wrapped in an edible lucent-crimson pulp with a unique tangy sweet-sour flavour.

PROSCIUTTO a kind of unsmoked Italian ham. Salted, air-cured and aged, it is usually eaten uncooked.

QUINOA (pronounced keen-wa) is cooked and eaten as a grain alternative, but is in fact a seed. It has a delicate, nutty taste and chewy texture, and is gluten-free.

ROCKET also called arugula, rugula and rucola; peppery green leaf eaten raw in salads or used in cooking. Baby rocket leaves are smaller and less peppery.

SESAME SEEDS black and white are the most common of this small oval seed; however, there are also red and brown varieties. The seeds are used in cuisines around the world as an ingredient and as a condiment.

SOUR CREAM a thick commercially-cultured soured cream. Minimum fat content 35%.

SOY SAUCE also known as sieu; made from fermented soy beans. Several variations are available in most supermarkets and Asian food stores. We use a mild Japanese variety in our recipes.

SRIRACHA is a medium-hot chilli sauce available from Asian food stores and some major supermarkets.

SUGAR
brown very soft, finely granulated sugar retaining molasses for its characteristic colour and flavour.
caster finely granulated table sugar.
white coarse, granulated table sugar.

SUMAC a purple-red, astringent spice, ground from berries growing on shrubs that flourish wild around the Mediterranean; adds a tart, lemony flavour. Available from most supermarkets.

TAHINI a rich, sesame-seed paste.

TAMARI a thick, dark soy sauce made mainly from soy beans, but without the wheat used in most standard soy sauces.

TOFU also called bean curd; an off-white, custard-like product made from the 'milk' of crushed soy beans. Comes fresh as soft or firm, and processed as fried or pressed dried sheets.

TURMERIC also called kamin; is a rhizome related to galangal and ginger. Must be grated or pounded to release its acrid aroma and pungent flavour. Known for the golden colour it imparts, fresh turmeric can be substituted with the more commonly found dried powder. When fresh turmeric is called for in a recipe, the dried powder can be substituted (proportions are 1 teaspoon of ground turmeric for every 20g of fresh turmeric).

VINEGAR
balsamic originally from Modena, Italy, there are now many balsamic vinegars on the market ranging in pungency and quality depending on how, and for how long, they have been aged. Quality can be determined up to a point by price; use the most expensive sparingly.
cider made from fermented apples.
wine made from either red or white wine.
rice wine a colourless vinegar made from fermented rice and flavoured with sugar and salt. Also known as seasoned rice vinegar; sherry can be substituted.

VANILLA
extract obtained from vanilla beans infused in water; a non-alcoholic version of essence.
paste made from vanilla beans and contains real seeds. Is highly concentrated: 1 teaspoon replaces a whole vanilla bean. Found in most supermarkets in the baking section.

WOMBOK also known as chinese cabbage or peking cabbage; elongated in shape with pale green, crinkly leaves, this is the most common cabbage in South-East Asia. Can be shredded or chopped and eaten raw, or braised, steamed or stir-fried.

YEAST (dried and fresh) a raising agent used in dough making. Granular (7g sachets) and fresh compressed (20g blocks) yeast can almost always be substituted one for the other when yeast is called for.

YOGHURT, GREEK-STYLE plain yoghurt strained in a cloth to remove the whey and to give it a creamy consistency.

ZUCCHINI also known as courgette; belongs to the squash family.

CONVERSION CHART

MEASURES

One Australian metric measuring cup holds approximately 250ml; one Australian metric tablespoon holds 20ml; one Australian metric teaspoon holds 5ml. The difference between one country's measuring cups and another's is within a two- or three-teaspoon variance and will not affect your cooking results. North America, New Zealand and the United Kingdom use a 15ml tablespoon. All cup and spoon measurements are level.

The most accurate way of measuring dry ingredients is to weigh them.

When measuring liquids, use a clear glass or plastic jug with the metric markings.

We use large eggs with an average weight of 60g.

DRY MEASURES

metric	imperial
15g	½oz
30g	1oz
60g	2oz
90g	3oz
125g	4oz (¼lb)
155g	5oz
185g	6oz
220g	7oz
250g	8oz (½lb)
280g	9oz
315g	10oz
345g	11oz
375g	12oz (¾lb)
410g	13oz
440g	14oz
470g	15oz
500g	16oz (1lb)
750g	24oz (1½lb)
1kg	32oz (2lb)

LIQUID MEASURES

metric	imperial
30ml	1 fluid oz
60ml	2 fluid oz
100ml	3 fluid oz
125ml	4 fluid oz
150ml	5 fluid oz
190ml	6 fluid oz
250ml	8 fluid oz
300ml	10 fluid oz
500ml	16 fluid oz
600ml	20 fluid oz
1000ml (1 litre)	1¾ pints

LENGTH MEASURES

metric	imperial
3mm	⅛in
6mm	¼in
1cm	½in
2cm	¾in
2.5cm	1in
5cm	2in
6cm	2½in
8cm	3in
10cm	4in
13cm	5in
15cm	6in
18cm	7in
20cm	8in
22cm	9in
25cm	10in
28cm	11in
30cm	12in (1ft)

OVEN TEMPERATURES

The oven temperatures in this book are for conventional and fan-forced ovens.

	°C (Celsius)	°F (Fahrenheit)
Very slow	120	250
Slow	150	300
Moderately slow	160	325
Moderate	180	350
Moderately hot	200	400
Hot	220	425
Very hot	240	475

Measurements for cake pans are approximate only. Using same-shaped cake pans of a similar size should not affect the outcome of your baking. We measure the inside top of the cake pan to determine sizes.

INDEX

PUBLISHED IN 2019 BY BAUER MEDIA BOOKS, AUSTRALIA.
REPRINTED 2019 (TWICE).
BAUER MEDIA BOOKS IS A DIVISION OF BAUER MEDIA PTY LTD.

BAUER MEDIA GROUP

Chief executive officer Brendon Hill
Chief financial officer Andrew Stedwell

BAUER MEDIA BOOKS

Publisher Sally Eagle
Editorial & food director Sophia Young
Creative director Hannah Blackmore
Managing editor Stephanie Kistner
Art director & designer Jeannel Cunanan
Senior editor Chantal Gibbs
Senior food editor Kathleen Davis
Operations manager David Scotto
Business development manager Simone Aquilina
saquilina@bauer-media.com.au
Ph +61 2 8268 6278

Recipe developers Carly Sophia Taylor,
Elizabeth Fiducia, Rebecca Lyall,
Domenica Reddie

Photographer James Moffatt
Stylists Kate Brown, Olivia Blackmore
Photochefs Elizabeth Fiducia,
Rebecca Lyall, Nadia Fonoff

Additional text Leanne Kitchen

Printed in China by 1010 Printing International

A catalogue record for this book is available
from the National Library of Australia.

ISBN 9781925695311 (paperback)

© Bauer Media Pty Limited 2019
ABN 18 053 273 546

This publication is copyright. No part of it may
be reproduced or transmitted in any form
without the written permission of the publisher.

Published by Bauer Media Books,
a division of Bauer Media Pty Ltd,
54 Park St, Sydney; GPO Box 4088,
Sydney, NSW 2001, Australia
Ph +61 2 8116 9334; Fax +61 2 9126 3702
www.awwcookbooks.com.au

INTERNATIONAL RIGHTS MANAGER

Simone Aquilina
saquilina@bauer-media.com.au
ph +61 2 8268 6278

To order books
phone 136 116 (within Australia)

or order online at
www.awwcookbooks.com.au
Send recipe enquiries to
recipeenquiries@bauer-media.com.au